THEY WERE MY HEROES

MOHUL BHOWMICK

ISBN 979-888606728-6

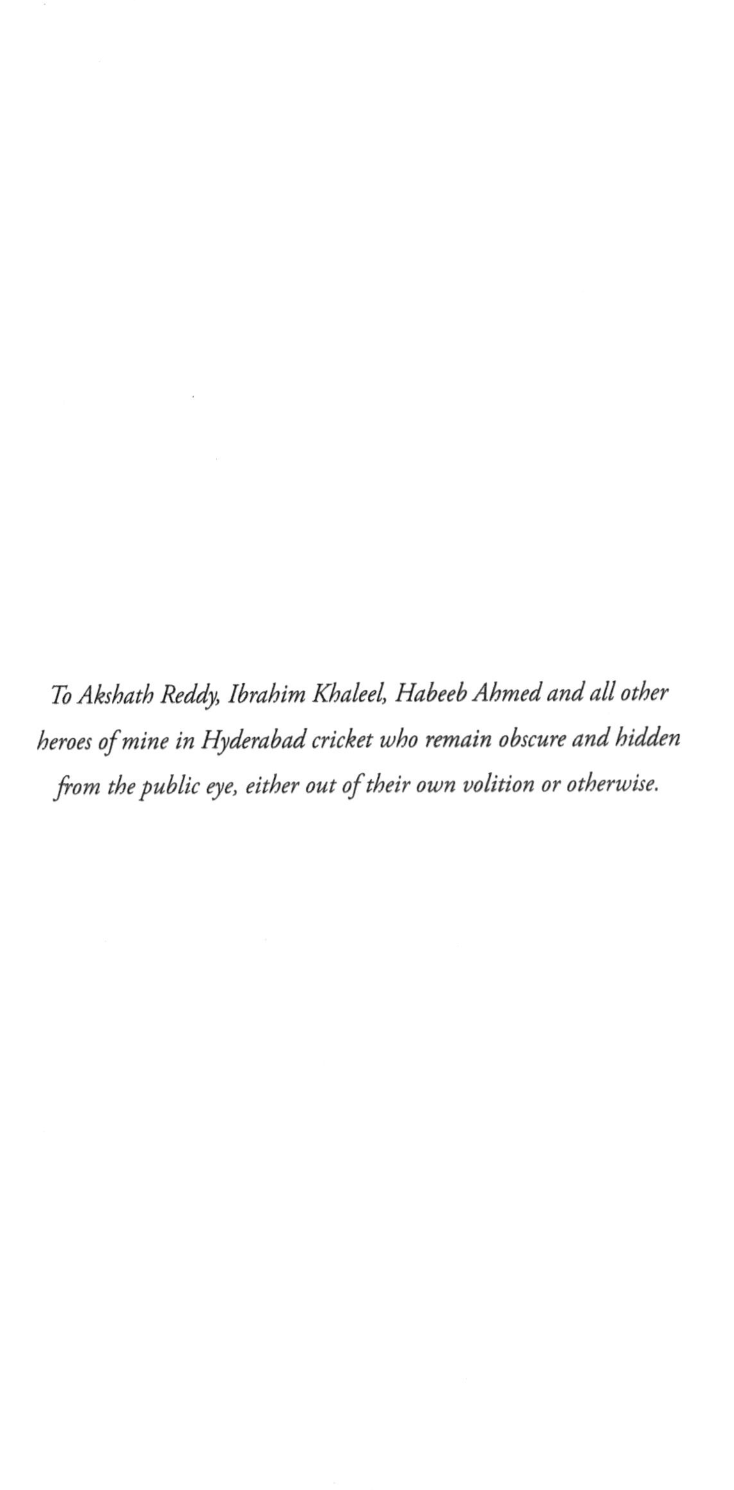

To Akshath Reddy, Ibrahim Khaleel, Habeeb Ahmed and all other heroes of mine in Hyderabad cricket who remain obscure and hidden from the public eye, either out of their own volition or otherwise.

Contents

Contents

Contents

Contents

Contents

Born in 1998, Mohul Bhowmick is a national-level cricketer, poet, sports journalist, essayist and travel writer from Hyderabad, India.

His debut collection of poetry *This Means War* came out in 2019 and was met with widespread acclaim. It managed to lodge itself and remain at number two in the Amazon Kindle Bestsellers' List. His most recent book, a travelogue on Nepal titled *Seeking Kathmandu* tasted similar success and has been celebrated widely in the world of travel literature.

He is also a post-graduate student of business administration at Bharatiya Vidya Bhavan's Vivekananda College, Osmania University, Hyderabad. He writes consistently for the e-magazine *LiveWire* and *The Times of India*'s blog.

Mohul harbours the dream of turning up for Manchester United at Old Trafford someday and playing the guitar alongside John Mayer at Wembley Stadium.

ALSO BY MOHUL BHOWMICK

POETRY
This Means War
An Audience Of One
Soaked To The Skin

NON-FICTION
Seeking Kathmandu: Travails of a solo traveller across Nepal

Preface

The conception of *They Were My Heroes* took place more than a couple of years ago, and it was only due to my newfound love in travel writing that it had to be pushed to the back burner. It took a while to get used to the term 'travel writer' being bandied about indiscriminately alongside my name by the mainstream media, but I knew that my heart lay in poetry and that this was where I derived the most joy from. I did not disagree with the great Hugo Williams when he said in an interview, "I need poems more than they need me."

I needed poems, and hopelessly so. They were the sole reality on which my existence, so to speak, flourished. I took to poems when I was feeling happy, and I took to poems when I was not. They had, by extension, become a part of my unmoulded character. How could I walk away from them? It would have taken a robust character to forsake the adulation that *Seeking Kathmandu* aroused; I am a fairly mild man, but my strength has been tested to its core. I can, however, affirm that I have been working earnestly as a travel writer and that a couple of fascinating projects find themselves on my desk.

They Were My Heroes is a veritable tome, as collections of poems go, and my longest book to date. I hope that the reader will appreciate my anxiety when I say that it was an onerous task to keep such a labour of love of over two years to less than a hundred poems. Several omissions took place in an already-burgeoning volume, and what you have in your hands now is possibly the lightest it could have been. I am just relieved that my commitments in cricket allowed it to be completed at all!

A lot of attention was paid to make sure that these verses resonated over time and space; rhyme and metre made themselves dulcet at every possible milestone. Poetry is designed largely to entertain- to give joy when one is suffering- and I fancy thinking that *They Were My Heroes* aspires to do so.

Mohul Bhowmick
Hyderabad
February 2022

"The legacy of heroes is the memory of a great name, and the
inheritance of a grand example."

- Benjamin Disraeli

Travel Capers

1. The Young Of Nepal

The young of Nepal live in crowded streets
While gyrating to Beyonce's beats.
They wear their hearts upon their sleeves
Protecting the rhododendron leaves
Which curl upwards and give them life
Sheepishly like a khukri knife.

The young of Nepal walk among trees
And, carried away by Phewa's breeze,
They live like there is no tomorrow;
That their life has seen no sorrow.
Their dal bhaat remains uneaten;
Fried momos do their palates sweeten.

The young of Nepal love without regret,
Spending it all till their desires are met.
They don't worry about the days of yore
As they have not seen them before.
The young of Nepal differ from the old;

Chasing which, in the past, they sold.

2. Annapurna

Annapurna, your precipices looked forbidding enough
Without that hostile glare that you gave to onlookers;
Your walls covered with knee-deep snow, your tongue
Lashed with the smile of loss, your lips curled in a
Laugh that was cruel than death itself; you painted
Quite the picture. The aversion could have been
Shrugged off and torn into pieces only if you were
Willing to, but it took me long enough to realise
That the hostility was only a pretence- that deep within
You welcomed us all into your lap.

A lap that was colder than the degree to which
Human faith could go. Annapurna, did you even realise how
Beautiful and ghastly you looked at the same time?
Your onlookers paid tribute after tribute to your eyelashes
While all I could see were the fangs that would engulf
Me in an avalanche that was only your creation; only
You could have been so hateful to those of your
Admirers. You asked them to go the extra mile, as
The French did in 1950, yet you were not satisfied;
You sent them tumbling down running away

From the animal that you had turned yourself into.
They named you after the Hindu goddess of food
And nourishment, yet all you gave were barren delights;
Only those who went close to you could have noticed
Your bare fangs, from 45 km away you seemed pristine
To a 21-year-old from Hyderabad who had only heard of
You and the challenge you posed to those who wanted
To go near you. You gave death to those who wanted
To touch you, and paradise to those who wanted to
Just know you. You did not want to be attained.

Annapurna, these days I wonder if you
Remember me or Maurice Herzog more fondly. He, who
Exposed your weaknesses and brought perennial shame
To your snowy flanks, or I, who watched you from afar,
Brooding and promising to myself that life wouldn't
Have been half as well-lived if I hadn't seen it from
The diagonally torturing corners of your balcony.
Or whether you still believe that I will come back,
Having made a name for myself and claiming the
Assurance you presented to me that day.

This poem was composed while gazing at Annapurna's marvellous structure but put into paper much later. A version of it appeared in the e-magazine LiveWire.

3. This Side Of Phewa

This side of Phewa is lined with the most
Exquisite rhododendrons that peer
At the endless blusters stretching out
In front of them. They peek at the vast empty
Nothingness with an impervious curiosity

That can give a five-year-old tough
Competition. Life of this side of Phewa can
Be tough but the gentle rise of the tide
Makes it seem easier than it actually is.
The sun rises from behind the gargantuan

Outlines of Machapuchare and Annapurna
While the clouds compete for space
With their petite, more insignificant
Compadres. The mountains puff their noses
In distaste in being made to compete

With hills who have no identities of their own
And decide to appear out of nowhere;
Just to spite you and those who now have
Their backs turned to Phewa. You are reminded
Of her existence again only when you look

To the west once the spell from
The enormity of the Himalayas is broken.
Phewa takes this in her stride, almost as if
She is used to playing second fiddle to
The Hercules that is Machapuchare.

The boats that line up on her sides
Remind you of the weakness with which
Misadventures of the youth are greeted with.
Phewa accommodates them all in her lap,
Welcoming the pious and agnostic alike.

The day goes by in a hurry and as the
Evening comes, Phewa's defences are breached.

Schoolkids and teenage lovers walk along
The promenade, neglecting and ignoring her,
So to speak. They speak in hushed voices as

The middle-aged reminisce of the days when
They were school kids and teenage lovers,
And Phewa winces when she remembers
Those days of yore. There are secrets
Buried deep within her tolerant soul.

You smile at her indulgently; she responds in kind
And before you know it, she has turned a
Deep shade of green that has nothing to do
With the resentment she has over her taller
Brothers who make her seem so insignificant.

4. If Pokhara

If Pokhara could take his senses by storm
And Lakeside's innocuous eyes
Breathed down his neck to taste the warm
Perspiration that smelled like ice-
Then he wouldn't have had to perform
This scanty offering to the skies.

If Pokhara spoke about leaving morals behind
The curtains of the doors of shame,
Then it was no accident, as he was to find
The sun going down the way he came.
Machapuchare called him over to remind
Of the home that he could not claim.

If Pokhara fed him lies and sold the truth
Of the way his soul was supposed to be,
He, in the carefree flush of youth,
Drove past redemption willingly.
He was no alien to the smooth

Satisfaction accompanying this debris.

5. If You Must Betray Me, Kathmandu

If you must betray me, Kathmandu, do it in the night.
When the day begins, you are understandably
Terrified of the tourists plaguing the insides
Of your intestines who make their way from
Gaushala down to the confines of the ring road
That ties you to the modern austerities of
Tribhuvan Airport. You had to be coaxed
To open your doors at six- in the morning.

When the day begins nothing remains except
The carcasses of the lepers who jumped
Out of the junipers that line themselves across
The thumbnail-sized windows of Old Baneswor.
This is where Manjushree Thapa's family home
Adorns itself with a garden filled with yellow leaves.
When you speak of yellowing leaves, Kathmandu,
Leave out those streets of Nag Pokhari

And those intensely confusing houses near Naxal.
It doesn't lend its name to the movement
That engulfed and almost burnt you down.
If you feel like a little self-love, go to Thamel
And watch with astonishing ease as
Man turns himself into Animal and pushes his
Chastity behind the dust of Jyatha's authentic
Thakali Bhancha Ghars. Or turn a blind eye.

Take the winding route down Ason and get on
The bus to heaven from Ratna Park. Begin
To marvel at the destruction that seems
To coexist in harmony with the bourgeoisie
That Thapa has enumerated well in her painful
Books. Twist my arms, Kathmandu, before beginning
The arduous trek north to Swayambhu and disregard
The images of what the world has known of you.

Forget Hanuman Dhoka and take the serpentine road
Before your inner self begs you not to go
Where you will be led astray; hop onto
My back as I lead you towards the bungalows
Of the maharajahs who exploited your

Generosity- who can't possibly loiter about
Narayanihiti if they had some shame. Pay
Your respects before you make the long trek

Up to Swayambhu on foot. I'll lend you my
Shoulders if you have the veracity to ask for them.
You are a paradox, Kathmandu, entrapped by
The naivete of your people and liberated by
Their tenacity. Flamboyance once made its
Home inside you near Maharajgunj but you
Threw her out the way she came from Tundikhel.
You could not be understood, yet you could be loved.

A version of this poem appeared in the e-magazine LiveWire.

6. On Chikmagalur

Where nature smiles in abundance by
The silver of the lake at night
And trees worship the orange sky
Watching the nightjar take its flight,
I wonder if it's the same in the dry
Towns at a much lower height.

How soon would life have to take a turn
Across the hills in this constant change?
Be careful not to let your hands burn
In the fire of the Budangiri range.
If Mulayanagiri makes you yearn
For something higher than this exchange,

Look no further than Ballarayana's eyes
And smile at it while you still can.
If the fort at the top takes you by surprise,
The wooded path on which you ran
Away from the burst of fireflies

Will tear apart your well-laid plan.

If Ayyankere makes you turn around
And Hirekolale stop and take a look,
Would Jhari have saved the ones who drowned;
Z Point punished every wanton brook?
Here, in these hills, these paths abound-
I hope you're glad for the road you took.

7. An Ode To The Western Ghats

The wind at the top of the mountain lingered.
What was the correct approach to throw us off-
Course? It wasn't the right time to climb
The peak of this grassy slope known simply
As the Queen's Point. We didn't know better than to
Tempt fate or ask the Gods above to challenge us
With the best that they had in their arsenal.

Nor did we assume that such a challenge would
Be taken up. Even when a fearsome wind
Started picking up pace from the park to our
West that housed Kudremukh and her sisters,
We paid no need. The fog that covered us
And the clouds that asked for permission
Lulled us into a sense of false security.

Nature smiled in abundance. The lantana
Bush that covered our approach waved without

Waiting for our consent. The leeches put off
Their hungry escapades until we had actually
Fallen down with all the grace of a Hyderabadi
Prima donna. The lone scorpion posed a feeler
To our unsuspecting boots, but we shrugged it off.

Kudremukh was covered in mist from head to toe.
As were her sister peaks, without exception. Milk
Gushed out of the waterfall in torrents that the dark
Clouds above us sought to emulate in earnest.
How difficult must it have been to lie in wait for the
Heavens overhead to unleash such fury upon
Our bare heads and gloveless fingers?

The embers of the fire inside us glowed with a
Reluctance that was customary of everything that
We tried to seek. Images of an infuriated peak
Remained in imagination. Sounds of a bloodless war
Conjured out of thin air. We rode the boat
Until the voices inside us were heard no more,
And the nightjar started calling out in panic.

Unsurpassed beauty passed us by without
Passing so much as a glance. Our eyes met with
The gushing waters of the stream that we had
Forded only minutes ago; there was no possibility
Of going back inside the dense undergrowth
That prevented our stuttering feet from moving
Further. Or was it due to the cries of the bull-frog?

The rain cascaded upon our raincoated backs
Without giving us any chance to disentangle
Ourselves. What had we done to anger the Gods?
Thinking ourselves to be lucky enough to evade
Being struck by lightning at the top of Queen's Point,
I looked on in dejection to the peak to our right rising
At an impossible angle, till you showed me its trail.

The mist hung on to the souls of the poplars as we
Wound our way back downhill. The roads screeched
With agony as the motor of our cycle crept down
Stealthily along the snake-like paths. The haze seemed
To close in on us, and even tried to choke us in its
Grip, coming so close as to make only the next

Few feet visible to our untrained, city-slick eyes.

Kudremukh curled its lips in derision. The waterfall
And the stream we forded exchanged meaningful glances.
The darkness seemed to engulf us bit by bit
As we tried to make good our escape from this
Heaven that had turned itself into purgatory. Whose
Sins were we carrying that left us soaked to the skin,
Naked except for our spirit in this ill-timed deluge?

8. Chandigarh

When you think of Chandigarh, think of the three
Amaltas that line the road on the way
Back from the serene confines of Sukhna. See
How they make room for the callous sway

Of your inhuman overtures. Look at one tree,
And feel its bark on a sunny day.
If you happen, at the moment, to think of me,
Do so after you avoid the spray.

If the fog clears up, or if you have the audacity
To go in summer (having lost your way)
I hope the Shivaliks welcome you at the knee
And serve you ice on a tray.

If the rock gardens overwhelm you with alacrity
And you wonder if you want to stay,

Think of the sun, and think of the free
Wind that carries you around all day.

• 23 •

When Sector 17 embraces you with a plea
To remain sober 'til your hair turns grey,
Hope you don't think too much and agree
To join in on this ballet.

9. Disagreements With Longing

I walk to the door with you- it was unusually cold-
As if the susurrated winds had somehow got hold
Of the conversation we left midway to strike
Clear of the edges we rounded and the
Vulnerabilities we exposed. So unlike
Both of us- as we stood in the darkness-

Quivering and not a little scared of the impending
Gloom. How chaste it must seem to you,
How false, how self-congratulatory too,
When you wrap your arms around the silhouette
Of the barb I have left behind; but no,
How could you long for that which would not last?

With every little fight that you had with
Light and its threatening obscurations, did
You not learn anything? How defenceless,
How unrecquited this may have appeared to you,

Shivering in the indifferent moonlight with
Dreams in my heart and desire in your eyes.

Of course, ignorant as we were, we didn't account
For the sharp zephyr that blows from east
To west in early summer in Coorg, which held
Sway over our misplaced passions that evening.
Whence could we have talked of the lovely
Remorse that settled upon your house?

How could we not have chosen to be more
Careful? The shopkeepers where you stopped
By to buy fresh produce welcomed me inside their
Doors thinking that I was attached to you somehow;
They seemed to have seen what you evidently
Did not, and rejected my lurking in the shadows.

What would this go down as, if anything, in the
Tiny diary you keep? I've heard from you once
Or twice by now- pictorial messages from places
You've been with people you've seen. Strangely,

There is only frigidity accompanying them, and
No voice saying, "Don't worry, I know you are there."

10. Bombay Tides

When Bombay called, and you left the room
To answer, I could have told that we were
Not going to make it. To be put through
Such exorcisms every time we put our clothes
On would have put an untenable strain
To our back-breaking and unamendable ways.

What was indeed commendable, at first
Was the way the entire bubble burst-
Of the allure of Bombay and its glamour,
Leaving out questions that led to clamour.
Indeed, the weather there was accursed
To have seen us at our very worst.

How such a deep, passionate appeal
For love could not have moved you I can
Never understand. To be able to move at once
From the penury of Borivali, with Malad
Rearing its head up from its own worries

To pay one's respects at Kandivali.

How could life have treated us this way
That we could not tell night from day?
What was so special in this city of dreams
That blood seemed to burst at its seams?
There was, in fact, not a lot to say
When those sunny eyes had turned to grey.

Both the halves of Goregaon seemed to
Merge in one before we had the sense
To understand that it was not really the case.
Santacruz could have shown its face but
Khar made sure that it did not have to.
We woke up to see Bandra at its finest.

Bombay had eyes at the back of its head,
Audacity making jaws drop by a thread.
Life seemed to have come full circle now
That to its vicissitudes, we could allow.
You could only visit, never sleep in its bed.

Get too comfortable, and you end up dead.

A version of this poem appeared in the e-magazine LiveWire.

11. Begin

Start at the bottom and you just might make it
To the top of this pyramid. Begin to marvel
At the faithless waters of time that transcend
Through your hands shivering at the magnitude
Of it all. Begin again to wake up to the cacophonies
Of Mehdipatnam and the tiny by-lane that
Leads to the bowels of Lakdi-ka-pul. Travel
Extensively through the minds of the ugly-jacketed
Tourists who line up in front of the Salar Jung
In anticipation of the bells to toll and the clocks
To turn. Walk past my uninhibited existence
With a vulnerability that could put intrepidity to shame.

In Tribute

12. If Rain It Must

If rain it must on your snowy peaks,
When will the wind stop howling
And turn these white precipices golden?
You continued to remain untouched by
The fanfare that enveloped mere mortals.

We had but a tiny idea about what you
Were trying to say- of what you were seeking
To achieve in a world that fed mediocrity
Deep into our stomachs. We didn't
Understand why you wanted to stand apart.

The hardest part was acting against the laws
Of self-preservation, almost as if you
Enjoyed denying yourself the gratifications
Of life that lesser men like us wouldn't
Have waited for a moment to succumb to.

We woke up to your greatest deeds
Being celebrated with unflinching pride,
Questioning how you'd been left unwounded by ego.
Other men below you had suffered,
Many had failed; all had believed.

If rain it must on your shaded hills
Piercing and dissecting every decision
That you had taken, merging the good with
The bad, often forgetting the 'why' behind them,
I hope you blink. While I catch my breath

From having run all the way to take in
The inheritance you left behind.
I keep forgetting to look at your face;
It seems crushed under the weight
Of the stories you would not live to tell.

If rain it must on your agnostic seas,
Maybe I will come swimming

Along your coast someday, wet to the bone
Trying to cognise your eccentricities;
Will you embrace me then or let me sink?

The last leaf from the withered tree
In your courtyard, prodding itself
To act against gravity, seems slow to
Embrace the sadness in the air while
Making its way gently to the ground.

In memoriam: Irrfan Khan.

13. A Eulogy: A Year On

A year has passed and the seasons have changed.
Your absence reminds us of the void
That was left behind after we were estranged.
When this dream is destroyed,

Your evincing notes still wake me at night
Asking me to forget yesterday's ghosts.
There's too much of YOU involved in this fight
So close on the edge of despair's coasts.

I hope they treat you nicely, I hope you're well.
You're bound to have etched a place
For yourself wherever it is that you dwell;
I can see that smile on your face.

A mixture of sadness and grief
Overcomes us when we hear your name.

We've never lacked this sense of belief
But truth be told, nothing is the same.

• 37 •

In memoriam: Mrs Abhignya Banerjee.

14. They Were My Heroes

Withered and shivering, sunken jaws,
Toiling in the heat without a pause.
Missing yet shooting innumerable arrows,
All of them were my heroes.

Broken dreams tearing them apart
With mildewy sadness in their heart.
Token of gratitude, a smile half-full,
Gravity having extended its pull.

Chattering teeth, yet so unguarded-
None of them knows how it's started.
Sweat adorning them in all its glory;
Such heroes try to tell this story.

On top of the opposition when it rains,
Their labour in plain view remains.

Never having surrendered, so adept,
At remembering all the promises kept.

Champa and Probir, in their own sweet way,
Engulfing the darkness that shadows day.
Humour and wit, with a twinkle in the eye,
Flippant with life till it passes you by.

Sir, with his class and dignity intact,
No foot out of place, teaching how to act
When you're alone in the face of strife.
Morals and integrity come to life.

Akshath, carrying Hyderabad on his shoulder
As the winds of fate couldn't get colder.
Battling alone, putting up a fair fight.
Him against the world- such a sorry plight.

Habeeb no longer flies up to third slip

But doesn't miss a chance to let it rip.
Undoubtedly the best, shining in the sun,
Showing how doggedness could be fun.

Punter, with his swagger and chewing gum,
No quarter given, and taken none.
Abrasive, abusive and in your face,
Quickly reminding that you've lost the race.

Season after season, year by year,
Pushing away all that they hold dear.
On good days, a 100, on most a few zeroes,
Without exception, they were my heroes.

The people mentioned in this poem, in chronological order, are my parents Champa and Probir Bhowmick; my guru the late Mr Anil Mittal; former Hyderabad captain Akshath Reddy; former Hyderabad wicketkeeper Habeeb Ahmed and former Australia captain Ricky 'Punter' Ponting.

15. A World Without You

MR ANIL MITTAL
11 JANUARY 1959 - 12 SEPTEMBER 2020

Holding my hand when the darkness came,
Calming me down when the hurricanes lashed,
You remained steadfast in every frame,
No matter how often my ideals crashed.

What was it that I did not learn from you?
Your name is synonymous with sweat and toil.
No matter how many I got or how few,
Your story is engraved deep into Hyderabad's soil.

There were heroes few in those days in the sun;
You topped the list with some flair.
Taking off with me in every race I've run,
I've felt your presence in every prayer.

The summer of '12 will remain with me
And I hope that it does so with you too.
Taking the glare off things when I was at sea,
Embracing me tightly when I had no clue.

The void you've left behind can never be filled;
Your voice is not to be heard again in this life.
I am what I am because of what you helped build-
Seeking the hard way out of this enduring strife.

To find myself at such a loss for words,
Sir, I never thought that this day would come.
Living perennially in the two-thirds,
I'm the sole dancer to the beat of your drum.

It felt like I could fly when I was standing by your side.
If I could be even half the man that you are in my eyes,
If I could face the darkest days and fight the tears inside,
The love we shared was eternal, how can I say goodbye?

Your head was held high from the day of your birth
Above immoral men whom you outran.
That the Gods themselves had to descend to Earth

To claim you as theirs and say, "Yes, this was a Man!"

A second father to me- I can't believe you're gone
And I don't want to live in a world without you.
I wake up with the hope of seeing you again at dawn.
Alas! Today, there are few men around like you.

A version of this poem appeared in the e-magazine LiveWire.

16. What Happens When They Dig The Grave?

What happens when they dig the grave
That they had made especially for you
And abandoned in the scorching heat,
In the process, letting it become less human?
To them, you had been the symbol of
Everything that they were not. It was no
Shock to me when they saw you leaving
This time; grace intact even in death.

How could I look at your face in that condition?
How could I not break down, tear the hair out
Of my scalp and blame whoever it was that had
Given such a cruel and untimely end to you?
How could I not cry?
Here I was wishing you'd tell me to stop, saying
That such maladroitness would not be acceptable.
Why, oh why, did you not rise and speak to me again?

I am sorry for the stains I left;
They turned out much darker than I thought they would.
But why were you silent when I wailed inconsolably
Drenching myself in the rain of a tomorrow that was
Never going to come? Why, oh why, did you not open
Your eyes for one last time before telling me it was
Alright, that all I had to do was survive the morning,
Keep the scoreboard ticking and get through to lunch?

Why did you not tell me that you wouldn't be here
Anymore to swim me through this deep sea
Full of bloody sharks? For all that you
Have prepared me for, I can never stoop down to
Their collective consciousness. Why did you not stop
Me from losing my composure and why, oh why, did
You not tell me to give as good as I got when they came for
you;
That your soul was not meant for them to be feasting upon?

In memoriam: Mr Anil Mittal.

17. Happy Birthday, Guruji

Happy birthday, Guruji on what would have been
Your sixty-second. You, who stood tall amidst the
Ruins and defections of the hot mess that
Hyderabad cricket had become, and you who
Understood me like no one else did, how can I
Ever repay this mountain of debt that I lodged up?

How am I supposed to believe that cardiac shock
Did to you what the likes of Abdul Azeem and Shahid Akbar
Could not? Love, which had always remained abundant
On your elongated shores, found a home inside this
Tiny heart of mine. How can I not miss you? The tales
Of having dislodged the best in the business
Remain unscathed even months after

You are gone, and although you did not like to
Speak of them the way you liked to speak of
My minuscule achievements, I knew deep
Inside my heart that you yearned to turn the

Clock back and walk out with the red cherry
In hand at the refurbished Fateh Maidan

Which bears no uncanny resemblance to
The Sirpur Mills Cricket Ground where you
Were supposed to make your debut.
I take great pride in the fact that you stood
There in the rain shielding me from the brickbats
Thrown both our ways. It was only you who

Believed in me when everyone was
Telling you to not sign me, and that included
Those at the club we both call home.
You risked your career for me and I know
This as well as you do. You waited with
Unending patience under the shade with

My father pleading you to have a
Sip of tender coconut water to prevent you
From getting a sunstroke, but you wouldn't budge until
I crossed the elusive three-figure mark.

And when I did, it was not the least
Surprising to see the two of you on

• 49 •

Their feet clapping with the
Enthusiasm of a couple of teenagers in love.
He gave birth to me and you were the thing
Nearest to that, and now that you are not
With me anymore, I wonder if anyone could
Ever love me the way you did. I sure failed to love you.

In memoriam: Mr Anil Mittal.

18. Escape

When days pass you by in a blur
And weeks zoom out of scene,
They remind me of what we were
And take me back to where we'd been.

How are you in the place you're in?
Does the pain ever subside?
Do your veins throb from within;
The rules of Life- do they abide?

Your passing has left a hole in my being;
I haven't slept a wink in weeks.
Creeping up on me unforeknown, unseen,
Is the scene of happiness' peaks.

When did you feel the grasp of Life
Slipping away and the Dark extending

Its cruel and mangled old knife,
Its rough arms in meekness bending?

You gave me joys I hadn't known before
Least of all which came before sunrise.
Who is it, I ask myself at the door,
But you're all I see when I close my eyes.

Sir, how can words describe what you meant
To me and all the lives that you shaped?
I ask myself where those years went;
Why couldn't this be a fate you escaped?

In memoriam: Mr Anil Mittal.

19. A Year Without You

The tears have not dried
And believe me, I have tried
To take this in my stride.
Yet, every time I think of you
I remember those just and true
Ideals. To breakthrough

Into someone's innermost
Thoughts must seem
Roughly pedantic, Almost
Being part of a dream.

I still remember the way I cried
And how I remained wide-eyed.
Who else was there to guide
This lost soul in a sea of blue?
And yet, together we flew
Away from this petty queue.

How do I go on living from here
When I have none of your charm?
Sure, the coast is now clear,
Nightingales calling out in alarm.

If you tell me now to bide
My time, I'll tell you of the slide
That has asked me to step aside.
Let's try to begin this anew.
I know for sure you feel it too,
My aching in this year without you.

There is no one like you, nor will be,
I can say this without a doubt.
The hand you've had in shaping me-
The featherweight in this heavy bout.

In memoriam: Mr Anil Mittal.

20. The Worthless Escape

Meaningless jokes as the night ends
Screaming tall tasks and lost friends.
Feeble attempts at the poetry of life
Turn into jostling for unending strife.

You're still smiling as time escapes
From hand and turns into brazen shapes.
There's no saying how this endless night
Can turn into a day unseemingly bright.

There's so little time, what's to be done?
Is there any way you not want to run?
There is vengeance in your eyes
As you simmer in your disguise.

Don't ask me my name, the game's just begun
An equal probability of either side to have won.

There's silence in these streets around you,
We could've been part of it only if you wanted to.

• 55 •

Misplaced memories come back just in time
Seeking ways for your visions to rhyme.
There's nothing more for you left to say;
Confiding in me about the beauty of today.

I can't stop looking into your eyes, they draw me in,
They ask me how and where I have been.
You've pulled me closer than your arms let,
Let's make this a night the two of us don't forget.

21. Remember Us

"Saab, remember us when you lift the curtain
Off your glass windows in the uncertain
Darkness that has descended on you.
As you fret, having thought this through,

We hope you remember to lock yourself in
Just as you locked us away from the din
Of safety. And good health. Don't begin
To get swayed by your conscience; no sin

Is committed; there's no blood in your hands
In the precipice upon which sympathy stands.
Forgive us for thinking that we could share
Your charity for which we made no prayer

To an unequal God. Don't get swallowed by guilt
As you stay secure inside the houses we built.

Between staying safe and staying alive,
We know not what awaits us as we arrive

On the other side. Life was not meant to be fair
To us, we only asked for some space to share
And to breathe your air. Now, as the second scare
Makes you retreat into your home, we walk bare

Footed towards ours, in a land where we're never
Thought of in more than numbers. This endeavour
Has made us see the light. Maybe you'll forget
Us but then you've always been in our debt."

A tribute to the tragedies that befell our migrant workforce during the lockdowns put in place to curb the spread of Covid-19.

22. The Darkness Of These Dust Clouds

May the darkness of these dust clouds
Hovering on us be soaked to the bone
While unveiling light from its shrouds
That we managed to outdo alone.

This battle will be won for sure
But hope is at a scarcity now.
Nothing like this have we seen before
Nor will we in the future allow.

What do you think of when the day ends?
Does it remind you of the unending sorrow?
Since when did we start to make amends
Being too scared of facing the morrow?

There's light at the end of this dark hall;

It kills us to see something as terrifying.
We're used to having our backs to the wall,
Victorious until the day we stop trying.

On Covid-19.

23. Such Heroes

Some heroes you're more than fond
And intend to create a lasting bond
Even if it means trying to sustain
The healing more than the pain.
But of course, if you must look beyond
Then you must do so again.

What have they given you but joy
And provided ammo to destroy
The fragile ego that attends
To your broken soul. Friends
Have long left you, but oh boy!
These heroes try to make amends.

If Anirudh was sheathed in his coat
Of flamboyance, Suman could gloat
Of things you've seen just in dreams;
He knows everything, or so it seems.
Ravi Kiran took you by the throat

While Anoop ripped you at the seams.

Alfred's a gentle soul- if there ever was one,
Vishal joins in the practical fun.
Bhandari has long since jumped the queue.
Danny's face is no longer as new.
Pavan displays dignity. Quadri has run
The race that ties them to you.

Manohar's past it now, but he doesn't show
Signs of stopping or at least going slow.
Ranga is the clown that everyone missed.
Ashwin is now lost to the mist.
Dhatrak was seen much long ago
With merriment that you dismissed.

Such heroes are rarely found today,
Try as you like, by the close of play.
Bravehearts of repute, lion among men
Who practice what they preach and then
Choose to walk away and downplay

That they can be trusted to do it again.

A tribute to the erstwhile State Bank of Hyderabad cricket team, now rebranded as the State Bank of India. The poem mentions, in chronological order, former Hyderabad first-class players Anirudh Singh, Tirumalasetti Suman, M Ravi Kiran, Anoop Pai, Alfred Absolem, Vishal Sharma, Akash Bhandari, Danny Derek Prince, T Pavan Kumar, Syed Ahmed Quadri, Daniel Manohar, P Rangaraj, the late Ashwin Yadav and Venkat Dhatrak.

Demons

24. Requiem

Now that there is nothing left but this,
Let me withdraw blandly into the backdrop
Of the walls that elude your touch, into
The expansive shadows that evade your grasp.
Let me acquiesce gently those forebodings
That enclosed themselves tightly around
Your silver-wrapped hair; I can now choose
To walk away from the light that defined
My existence and deified my belongings.

There's a peculiar smell of freedom in my eyes.
I can now look at the forsythia outside
My neighbour's dust-rimmed window without
A trace of sin or hint of unease. My need
Has strangely worn away after the revelation
Of a new challenge, more so after the vision
Of you in the grime-filled chambers of fantasy's
Hall of fame; acceptance did not linger deep,
Sheltering me in the umbrae of doleful dreams.

My hands will rot, as will my memory at the
News of your imminent arrival; no coming and
Going will stand the quiz of time's salt-coloured
Tides. These words we declaim, these thoughts
We escape from- they will wither away
Into the hour of rust that shall settle in once
The moment of grandeur passes. No longing for
The touch of the warmth of your fingers on my
Reluctant skin will be heeded to, nor taken up.

It seems to me that I had conceived this poem
So long ago that I can not follow its ending now;
Quite like him, I have to find a way to begin anew.
All the ripples on my desire's waves will begin
To understand why this withdrawal was necessary;
Why, for the time being, there had to be something
That occupied the flesh of my feeble mind with
The colour of magnolia and the song of nightingales.
"Forgetting was indeed easier," you used to say.

The morning passes me by without dropping in
To say hello; the perfunctory nod of well-meaning

Approval does not enter my door anymore. The
Afternoon's lingering weakness makes me stoop
From the high halls of lyrical exultance I have built
For myself. As for the evening, this life has made me
Admit that whatever I do shall remain embedded
In the sands of posterity, the hubbub of the water
Underneath my fingers being the only constant.

My eyes will lose focus, your understanding
Will decay; we will be reduced to being mere
Footnotes in a history we had claimed to create. No
Pain or foreboding will profess its acquaintance
With the shock you felt when life was ticking away.
No future, however bright, will step into our
Windows looking in rather than looking out.
These exalted doors full of ignoble absurdity
Will join hands with the obscenities of faith.

Every touch was deemed unavoidable, at least
Till righteous indignation filled our fingertips
Without any evidence of time's scars. There may
Not be any scenic tragedy that accompanies my
Retreat towards the clouds; how unfortunate must

I have to be, like Zafar, to be denied being cremated
Beside my beloved Gymkhana. There can be no
Escape from these chains I built, not until there
Remains any trace of you in my memories.

25. When Regret Visits

Sometimes I can't sleep at night
Fearing memory's diatribe.
Soon darkness engulfs the light
Which I try to circumscribe.

I shiver to see my sorry plight
Wavering upon my shaken skin.
A part of it had once been bright
Though now it's dead from within.

Why can't I shake these visions dead?
Why can't I sleep like I used to?
When my life is hanging by a thread,
Why can't I just forget that view?

The night crawls as slowly as I do.
I'm close to death in my head.

There, really, is no clue
As I force myself to look ahead.

These moments lash a storm
And crush me with audacity,
But soon the will to outperform
Is hampered at capacity.

It's morning- the sun will soon arrive;
I try to evade it all the more.
It feels good just to be alive
Urging memory to close its door.

26. In Delirium

The hands of the clock are set in their ways
Displaying the time that was seen much before
A calamity of this size erupted; they stare at me

In mock annoyance as they oscillate between
Deciding whether to keep up with this pathetic
Charade or accept themselves for what they are.

I raise my hands in mock surrender
As I sidestep from being pulled into another
Conversation of who was right and who wasn't;

They give me the glare of someone who feels
That they have been wronged. I ignore all such
Hostilities and focus instead on the morning

Newspapers with no date which appear
To bring the truth out and remind the world
Of its fallacies with excruciating slowness.

The owner of the hands of the clock stops
Me on the edge of the street and wants
Me to understand its significance right then and there.

****

For how long must this long-drawn battle of will
And skill be stretched? The right word never
Seems to step inside my mouth as I wave

Frantically as you float past my shortcomings;
You rush back inside, to all our chagrin
Having to confront the cruelties of life.

I evade the dexterities of this confusion
Like an expert boxer does to those of his competitor's
Undercuts. Unlike Williams, might it be too early

To do something useful with my life? I decide not
To take sides with myself as my eyes finally
Begin to talk to me while avoiding my gaze.

27. False Pretence

It might be easy at first
Taking sides with myself,
Being led astray by the fireflies
Which seemed to be the light
At the end of this tunnel.

It might even be reassuring
To forgive myself from time to time,
Wondering where the road
That I left unequivocally
Would have led to.

It would seem hard later on
When the crowds have gone,
The photographers and the journalists
Seemingly not caring
About my existence anymore.

It would get more arduous
When the lines are drawn,
The swords have been sharpened
And the edge of my voice
Finally found its home.

The idea of the truth I'm chasing
Seems too good to be true,
But it is pleasing at times
To deposit faith in myself
And have it repaid in full.

28. The Newspaper

The day begins on the edge of the sidewalk;
I leave it at the bottom of the hill,
Cross over to the other side and repeat the act.
The rest of the morning passes by keeping my
Fingers crossed as I speak my heart out.

When it starts, it sparks of being fresh off the mill
Outpouring its joy at reporting others' misfortune.
I wince as I pour it a cup of tea only out of
Courtesy and reluctant acceptance at what it
Has achieved; it does not return my smile.

The clock stops chiming once it realises
That its significance is lost upon me;
It instead turns its attention to more
Pressing matters that have taken its breath
Away with more hoopla than I ever did.

By the afternoon it is crumpled with stale news.
I give it the once-over although the yews
Still stink with the odour of remembrance
And its more elastic companions; the yellowed
Pages grimace as I fold them back neatly again.

In the meanwhile, it competes with the pretty
Anchor on TV who has misunderstood the meaning
Of being impartial; it responds by pushing the
Photographs of a semi-nude struggling actress
Onto the page beside number three.

By the evening it has lost all interest in me.
The parched, wrinkled piece of paper that it now
Resembles is a far cry from what it will be
When I pick it up again tomorrow;
I lie down in anticipation.

29. On Turning Twenty-Two

Where is the joy that was seen yesterday?
Where is the sunlight peeking through?
Why is it that I am left with hell to pay,
When, to my God, I've just bidden adieu.

From now on, what will life look like?
Will the sun still rise tomorrow?
It hides away from me lest I strike,
Seeking to end this continual sorrow.

How do I exist in a world where He does not,
How do I live my life from here on?
I won't let this stain become a blot
Though this battle appears long-drawn.

Is this the present that Nature is giving me?

Or am I being made a fool by Time again?
At Twenty-two, is this the man I want to be?
If only He could see how I've fought the pain.

30. After The Bouncer

It appears at first to be an innocuous-looking delivery,
Acquainting itself with the width of the surface,
Glazing it lightly and rearing up without any shame
Up to a height that possesses no respectability at all.

You're stuck midway between going forward and back
In a state of mind airline pilots call 'the point of no return.'
You hope fervently for it to die down and for this to be
A false alarm, but it comes on to you quicker than you expect.

It is over within moments- the darkness that engulfs you
And the collective 'Oohs' that go across the field.
You fall onto the ground, lucky to have not disturbed the piece
Of wood situated exactly behind you, but the world starts spinning.

You're later told that the piece of leather smacks
Right onto where your bone meets skin- a graft of Godly
Presence prevents you from being permanently blinded
As the temple above your right eye takes most of the blow.

You remember nothing from the time when you'd last seen it,
And now the same innocuous-looking delivery is nestled
Softly within the hands of the square-leg umpire,
Who asks after you, as do the rest of the folks

You're competing with. But not the thrower of this particular
Javelin who's comfortably leering at you from the halfway
Mark, admiring his handicraft at having made one of the
Best pullers in the city squirm from the venom he has spewed.

It is hard to suspect that he is not satisfied with himself,
Although outwardly he may display an image of compassion.
It is harder still, to not feel sorry for yourself for the condition
That you find yourself in; no, this moment of self-pity must
pass!

Some of your teammates laugh it out as the physio asks you
Questions the answers of which you learned in elementary
school.
You're glad that there's no sign of the colour red in your
flannels-
It won't bode well for them to see that there's been blood
drawn.

You reassure yourself just as the physio asks if you'll be
Able to carry on- an aspirin and an icepack change hands,
As does the steely look of timid courage and intrepidity
That is generated from your now-swollen temple and right
eye.

You take guard again and shudder at seeing the red cherry
Located safely in the hands of the bowler at the top of his
mark.
He rushes in at you in a buzz of otherworldy excitement,
Trying to make the most of this moment of panic he has
induced

As feelings of impotence fill your entire being.
You question your self-worth, you question your right
Of being there- you question everything that is there to
question
In the ten seconds it takes for him to reach the popping crease.

But this time, you've chosen to not listen to those voices
And with your front foot extended and head on top,
This particular innocuous-looking delivery is dispatched
Through extra cover with the grace of a certain Indian number
three.

The thrower of this imbecile pellet grunts in disgust
And gives a shriek of repugnance as a collective sigh
Gathers momentum and spreads across the crowd.
You smile at him; he does the bare minimum to return it.

A version of this poem appeared in the e-magazine LiveWire.

31. On Rejection

Rejection hits you like a bus
And leaves you bruised in places
That you didn't know existed
In your own body; it snatches
Your mental peace, races alongside
Your shadows to question your
Very existence in this world and puts you
In situations where you are forced
To make hasty, tactical retreats.

Rejection climbs up to you as you
Breathe and forces itself down your
Throat as you try to swallow whatever
Little pride you have left. The feeling
Of aversion lasts longer than the feeling
Of infirmity as rejection makes you
Choke and force-feed the ego that you
Had so willingly vomited. Life smiles
Gently at your predicament,

But rejection follows around everywhere
You go, pushing itself to the top of the
List of the things that you want to get undone.
You try to sever all cords with it, only
To end up being tied to it for even
Longer. It throttles itself around
Your soul and sucks out its remnants
With great taste. You're not surprised
To see that it finds it to its liking.

Rejection follows you around
As you start to walk in circles,
Forcing the courage hidden inside
Your shallow self-esteem to rise.
Rejection makes you answer
Questions that would not have needed
Answering otherwise, and although
It stings tremendously, you make
It through one night, and then another.

Rejection makes you look inwards
And assess everything that is wrong

With you and not them, and
Celebrate the fact that it is only
YOU who can endure, who can take it.
It is pointed out to you that
If it were not for rejection, you would
Not have existed in the first place,
Nor earned the right to fight.

32. Not January Yet

That time of the year when you're looking ahead
To the promise that tomorrow will bring
Forgetting how often it was you bled
Or were left hanging on a tiny string.
At least you haven't lost the right to sweat-
It's dark but it's not January yet.

You've been hurt often, but you've not fled
Looking for pastures outside this ring.
You haven't become what you used to dread
And that fact has not clipped your wing.
It was worrying for a while- now it's no threat;
It's cold but it's not January yet.

The new year promises sunrises a shade of red
While to the years of yore you cling.
Does it really matter what they have said,
Or what they've been made to sing?
This year has not your expectations met;

It's gloomy but it's not January yet.

Infrequently you've been left for dead;
All you did was keep track of your thing.
Of quitting, you have come close instead-
There's a lot of life in this coming spring.
You know your mind is your biggest asset;
It's dismal but it's not January yet.

33. The Heart Of Life

Life is a circle that goes round and round,
And takes you with it in its afterglow.
The truth takes a hit and rumours abound,
And the sun is overtaken by the snow.

You are lucky indeed to not drown,
When the tides of time rise and flow.
You panic a little when you hear the sound
Of the winds of change when they blow.

It's been told to you that the heart of life is good
And it works out well in the end.
You regret those countless chances that could
Have turned your foe into a friend.

Be careful to give your heart, and if you should,
It might not be as you intend.

You've walked past the spot where you stood
Past those souls you tried to mend.

Life seems worthwhile minus the greed,
Which helps your intention to run.
And though you've been left to bleed,
You know the race has just begun.

Don't try to amass more than what you need,
Accumulating them purely for fun.
This wasn't the condition to which we agreed;
The battle with your mind that you won.

When you love, do so without any doubt,
Don't let shadows creep inside.
This may not all be what it should be about;
You just have to take it in your stride.

Don't stifle your lungs when you want to shout;

When it hurt you every time you cried.
One shot you get at this, so throw inhibition out,
Glorify the night when your old self died.

• 91 •

34. The Before And The After

The before is laced with the excitement
Of 'doing it' and being the first ones at it.
It is tied with passion and an
Overwhelming need to 'express yourself.'
It is filled with shaking knees and sweaty palms
But an overriding want to extend yourself.

The after is filled with a sense of guilt
And regret that has crept its way slowly
Inside the confines of the left side of your brain.
It is loaded with a tinge of concern and the sight
Of 'what if' and punctured with bits and pieces
Of the wounded ego that you had once possessed.

The before is all bright and shiny
With everyone around telling you how wrong
It would be to not 'do it.' It has no understanding
Of shame or how the world's schisms petrify

And knock the living daylight out of your only
Soul. The before is overly expectant.

The after has seen what has happened
And sneaked inside its shell for want of something
Better to do. It has understood the harshnesses
Of pain and reluctantly been so refractory
Up to the extent that blaming it has somehow
Felt wrong. The after is dark and twisted.

The before is a model of what can happen
If you let your mind wander away from the
Boundaries that you had set for its unloving
Sisters. It is childish and believes in
Ghosts and Santa Claus and winters in Hyderabad.
The before is filled with exaggerated exhilaration.

The after looks for people to blame
And unsurprisingly, finds nothing outside
You to hang on to. It peeks with no

Outward enthusiasm at the condemned
Before sentencing you to the guillotine
Just as you were about to take a little bow.

35. Entrance Of A Star

The field is set, the rest of the players make
Their way back to where they were standing earlier
While the one new to the crease hesitates slightly
Before turning towards the other end.
Those closest to him anticipate something big
Coming their way but his ubiquitousness
Hardly ruffles a feather. The assurance he portrays
That he is here to stay with the presentation
Of the full face of his bat along with the sound
Of solidity echoing through the green fields full
Of sunshine and well-earned respect allows the
Fielders to go back to where they were standing
And count down to when they can break for tea.

The stage is set, the displays of unwarranted
Machismo calls for loud shouts of "Encore" from the
Crowd but this is before they realise that the
Starlet of this show has not made his bow yet.
The people in the crowd watch with luscious delight
As curtain call after curtain call of avant-garde
Performers fill the night with unfiltered pleasure.

Then, almost as if he is too embarrassed to break
The reverie created by his fellows in the same show,
Our man makes his way unaccompanied by any of
Fame's in-laws on to the stage. By the time the night
Has ended and the crowd roared its approval,
He has found himself in the middle of nowhere…

36. Can't Give You Up

What starts no more than a gentle trickle
Leads to things often left unnoticed.
Sleep is the biggest casualty in this battle,
With footnotes on the subject of desire.
Young again in the advent of the morning,
Replenished enough to go soul-searching…

Servitude seeps into the mind with
Groundless thoughts running amok
In the sensitive fields of lucidity.
You're often the last man standing,
And love is too weak a word to have
Kept you sated in this tug of war.

We have both reached a kind of succour
That the years can claim to have created.
I am therefore unjaded and jaundiced
To such an extent as to know
That the universe has claimed this as a win.

We're not there yet, and I can't give you up.

Weathered by the storms of defeat;
Beaten in its tracks by forlorn longing;
Defeated by the indecencies of destiny;
And encouraged by victories over time.
Inured by rebuffs across the years,
Accumulating the drug named hope.

37. A Song For My Soul's Reawakening

It's difficult to fall asleep at night
Without the sound of lullabies.
As thoughts permeate within my sight,
A weight falls upon my eyes.
Whence did this simple joy become
A task rendering my heart numb?

Why do I shriek at the very mention
Of all that scared me in the past?
Now that they have my full attention
They're trying to make it last.
For as long as I process sound
I flail like the man who drowned.

Unadulterated joys no longer fill my day
Nor do thoughts of pure delight.
Uninvited pleasures haven't come my way;
I struggle to see my sorry plight.

When did I become a man I despise?
My ego visits me in disguise.

It's not time for me to pack my bags;
This, sure as hell, I know.
Unclaimed territories on which my flags
Are yet to flutter and blow.
It's not you who will tell me when to leave;
There are sensations left to achieve.

Don't leave my side, don't go just yet
And leave at my mercy.
I am free and in no one's chains or debt,
Devoid of controversy.
Stopped by the wayside, those who began
This journey with me, down to one.
I have some fuel and another plan
To end this race as the one who won.

A version of this poem appeared in the e-magazine LiveWire.

38. The Infusion Of Light

Crossing the river determined on deceiving
This tempest, and avoiding being thrown
Overboard, or trying at the very least,
You and I have turned the clock back

Rounding the curve to find ourselves
Back where we had begun. Being starved
Of the affection that we thought should never
Have been denied to us, we looked up

To the heavens and a God whose
Lashings had borne the marks of pockmarked
Brutality with ridiculous alacrity; we could
Indeed have chosen to ignore the sunset.

We were subdued by the floggings of time
And ambushed by the chains of the evocative

Summer air. These words had barely
Escaped my tongue that you chose to walk

Away from the timidities of Billy's
Narrow-minded rain. There should have been
A greeting, or a smile, or something other than
The muted laughter of ego's tear-stained walls.

Traffic yelled from the street below us
As our shadows noticed the gates being shut;
Yet we could have opened any door,
Entered any room the evening offered.

39. Wonderance

Stand in a field long enough, and you'll listen
To the thistles swaying by the buffeted air
That reeks up to your ankles and asks your name.

Wonder at the impenetrable silences that
Used to evade the responsibilities we took up;
Perhaps there were far too many signs of hate.

There was a lone door putting off our attempts
At breaking inside the void created by the
Silences of tragedy; this was no comic timing.

It used to be warm in April when the sun beat
Down in all its force upon those of us still
Standing imperturbed by such delusions.

Where ever have those timid companions of life
Taken their suitcases to? The off-putting rain that
Unpalatably accompanies us tonight says nothing.

40. In Tributo, Beard

I step up to the plate with a bowl in hand,
Soften the thistles with annoying bristles.
As of yet, things are still as planned,
Wary of missiles in life's dismissals.

The clipper comes out first, not wary or shy,
Tearing things apart, gently part by part
'Til I look at myself with someone else's eye.
With an unsteady start, I jolt my heart.

It drones on till no decencies remain
Bidding 'bye to my three-month-old ally.
A strange sensation, akin to breaking a chain.
I can't deny- I need this cream that I apply.

Now the foam takes over in all its glory,
The razor brings with it a new spring.

This can be a fresh start to my face's story,
An old wing but it's still the same thing.

41. Old Scrapbooks

In your aching hands, I see
Hurt you don't want me to feel.
Collected in your memory
Are the tears you try to conceal.

The old scrapbooks that remain-
If they come into your view,
May the photos spare the pain
Of joy they once brought to you.

42. Pegasus

When Pegasus, the pigeon, not the horse
Had flown his nest, we, of course
Did not know whether to cry
Or scream that he learned to fly
Without any push from those coarse
Cousins of his who, by and by,
Showed him images of the petulant sky
On their phones, taking our WiFi source.

They told him that life was too short
To not know how to fly. He developed a sort
Of cryptic smile towards the end
Of his days with us. He was a friend
Whose existence started as a tiny import
From his mum who decided to spend
Her pregnancy with us and defend
Him within the battlements of our fort.

She chose the balcony of the Bhowmicks' flat

And made a nice home of it, at that.
She moved in search of healthy trout
And poked in and out with her snout
Till Pegasus thrust from the egg that
Survived all the jostling and the doubt.
We wondered why he was so stout
More than any pigeon- he was no acrobat.

Took time finding his legs- the little one,
His cousins wondered if he'd jumped the gun.
Tried to make his life harder by being there
Not doing anything than sit and stare
At his futile attempts to join in the fun.
Flapping his feeble wings in the air,
One day it became all too much to bear.
A leap turned to flight, and his battle was won.

A version of this poem appeared in the e-magazine LiveWire.

43. The Shade From Our Tree

If time was the greatest gift
Given to Man and his tribe,
Then all the while he'd been adrift
Would have had him imbibe

Empathy- lots of it- to the core
And asked for his calling card.
Instead, it bothered him no more
And ran away after being scarred.

If ever there comes a shift
In the ideals to which you subscribe,
Hopefully, it won't create a rift
Between you and your diatribe.

The powers which I'm working for

Have not impeded, nor barred
Me from walking on this floor
But taught me to be on guard

Against the duress of those who sift
Through memories and proscribe
Virtues we saw on the makeshift
Staircase you had to circumscribe.

I'll ask you to gently open the door
And replace illusions with the charred
Photographs that survived the roar
And scatter them in the yard.

Whatever it is that sets me free
From what it is I'm supposed to be,
I'm sure I'll never get to see
This residual shade from our tree.

I'm hoping that you'll get to know
The way the winds of change blow.
From every high to every low,
It's kept your insides still aglow.

44. To All The Watches That I've Worn

All the watches that I've worn have
Shown me more than just time.
They've grown into a part of my soul,
Becoming truly mine.

Customs of fashion and of style
No matter how grand
Have evaded my wristy friends
Reeking of sweat in their band.

So much that they have chosen to adapt
My manners by and by.
Although they faced great objections,
They did not stop to try.

Now it's come to me trying to choose

Between them and the hat
That this language deplores us to wear.
(You didn't understand that?)

It's a dark addiction, deeply satisfying.
For junkies, it's complex.
Titan, Timex and more such in the past,
Casios now- soon a Rolex.

45. A Prayer For Strength

To all the powers that govern
These hands and feet of mine,
It becomes your concern
When you confine

This battle-ready soul
That has shown strength.
May you get to be the sole
Heir of its peace at length.

May you lead me towards Light,
Ending this state of mind.
You're not liable for my plight
When I try to leave behind

The pull of forces of evil pure
And dishonesty in a jar.

I'd merely like you to assure
That I won't have to stretch as far.

If I seek justice by day
And sleep with Truth at night,
I don't think you get to say
That I have lost the fight.

Is there any need for prediction
Of my progress in this quest
If I go to bed with conviction
That I have done my best?

46. The World's Most Priceless Drug

Of all the petty delights in life,
Few beat a hot shower.
Cutting all anxiety with a knife,
It strides in the golden hour.

Enveloping you like a vice,
Arms reaching for attention.
Joy doesn't come for a price
Nor cure precede prevention.

If you've been lucky to have one
That feels like a warm hug,
Then feel free to jump in for fun
At the world's most priceless drug.

47. Monsoon Lament

These leaves fall without your permission.
These wanderings and these inhibitions
Evade your grasp and float mercilessly
Into the vacuum created by my absence.
These impediments that you display

Are restrained by the colour of silk on your
Skin and condemned by the very touch
Of the floating currents of my words. I hope
To escape into the realms of the otherworld
Without your knowledge or clutching at straws.

The shadows fall fitfully into the evening
Light that filters in through the darkened
Corners of my mind. No wonder has ceased to
Amaze me as much as your disapproval at my
Lustre being lost in this bedlam you created.

What could have brought two kindred souls
Together more quickly than this censure
Of everything that went beyond our noses;
You choosing to neglect everything that was
Surpassing your widespread boundaries

And me trying to forge an identity of which
I had been no author. What of the unfettered
Chains of misconduct that crept their
Way up to the vast arenas of incoherence
In your absence, or the reluctant truths?

These walls leave opinions that delve
Deeper into the contours of my mind than
The feeling of imagined circumstances
Ever did. This transient moment of lost
Time seeks its way out of the mess I made.

What of the dew that falls upon the prying
Leaves of poplar in this inaudibly unfulfilled

Monsoon? What of the dust clouds that fall
Into the earth with a vengeance that often
Bears their unwillingness to cohabitate?

The shoulders of this tired mind are congested
With relentless drizzles of an unfaithful stupor,
As are its hands cloaked in a shrinking slice
Of courage often masquerading as the lone
Knight of truth and honour this evening…

Who bears responsibility for the tears that
You do not shed, or the fears you do not get
To whisper? Who questions this tremendous
Inability of ours to pass this night by without
So much as a murmur while the moon says hello?

Goodbye to the words that made you stop
And look me in the eye, and goodbye to all
The fancy mutterings of hope and faith
That took you by surprise; I am ready now
To revel in the shame of tonight's rain.

48. The Things I Left Behind

Having been denied the luxury to grieve,
Losing the ability to believe
In oddities that surpass the human mind
Are all the things I left behind.

Don't try to question me if I desire
To return home and stoke this fire.
It's not too late to see the light;
It would help if it were not so bright.

I bypass life's instructions with ease.
Its wrath is brought to its knees.
I promise I won't ever stop to see
The monster it turned out to be.

49. Without Me

How long is this fleeting life for?
How often must I live this lie?
The taste of blood in this timeless war
Evades me the more I try.
No matter how often I sigh
And point out the things I abhor,
The falsity of what I adore
May have no nest left to fly.

You can see man bound in chains
By the promises he failed to keep
From the dusty bylanes
Of guarantees that came so cheap.
When you take a minute to weep
About the debris and remains,
Weep till the sway of virtue reigns
Around the hills that seem asleep.

The rigours of joy and pain

Escape sense when you wish to see
Whatever it is that's left to gain
Space in our collective memory.
Whither have we floated in this sea
Of miseries and disturbing rain?
Surely the fight would not go in vain
When you cross over without me.

50. To Dispel This Gloom

If autumn leaves were to fall anew
And we could start afresh again,
Would you still look at the few
Dewdrops on your windowpane?

Would you still choose to love
And wash the pools of pain away?
Or does hurt still lurk all above
Other emotions at the end of play?

How ignominious it must seem
To forego such joy at the very sight
Of grief. Does the Sun ever scream
Or run away when it's dark at night?

If you were to be offered a boon
Of flowers withered yet in bloom,

Would you miss the silver moon
That's risen to dispel all this gloom?

51. Imbalance

Like the summer rain that fell
And the taste of freedom in my mouth,
It wasn't easy to foretell
When our fortunes would go south.

Life's perambulations have us in its eyes
And our faith held in its vice-like grips.
Woe betide if you're taken by surprise;
More like British stiff upper lips.

Why would you choose to walk away
From running into the midday sun?
If, later, you crumble and choose to stay
You might find the day is done.

It's never been in our best interest
To poke fun at destiny, tempting fate.

So in spite of what he seems to suggest,
Profanity's not up for debate.

The blood in the kitchen sink has waned
Its flow where it gushed from.
Your courage seems to have gained
To take things as they come.

There are, as a rule, few choices in life,
Just as there are fewer gifts.
Yet when such feelings are rife
Do make sure the balance shifts.

52. September

Has it all gone to waste?
Now that summer's moved on
With autumn greatly debased.
The starless gaze of early dawn
Looks quite timid when faced
With the fact that time has gone.

No chase could ever matter more
Than the one I perpetually took.
Upset dreams come to the fore
And have us all brought to book.
The flogging of this downpour
Makes me stop, turn and look

To the untimely, premature death
Of a centipede in this bloodless war.
Do not waste your breath
Trying to break this door.
Neither Wordsworth nor Seth

Can swim us to the shore.

It's awfully fitting that the last
Day of September bids goodbye
This way. No pain is broadcast
Nor joy at this vicious battle cry.
The flag is no more at half-mast;
There are no options left to try.

Searching for what's already gone
Makes a mockery of the truth.
Reduced to being a mere pawn
In the indolence of our youth,
Makes this more long-drawn.
If only there were words to soothe

The hardened soul I carry around,
I would've bandied them about.
Now, nearing the end of the round
Carousel of this dream, I shout.
Towards eternity is this pursuit bound

Far from the chasms of doubt.

53. An Immoral Dilemma

Happy enough to remain a passive bystander,
Unhaunted by the memories of the past.
Unhinged, unfettered by the moral wherewithal
Of making immortality last.
No longer in the wings of destiny's cruel winds,
Twigs falling as the flag's half-mast,
Life absorbs every remaining bit of dignity.
No wonder the sun is aghast.

Wolfed down by eminence, consumed by vanity,
Devoured by this thing called pride.
How long must this charade go on, this hypocrisy
Unmarred by the things you try to hide?
Loved to perfection, if only just, ended in time
Before the paint could have dried;
Forgetting the pain and hurt of the moonless dawn
Who housed you when you cried.

What does it take to shield your baby-faced innocence

And the incidentals that come for free?
What does it mean to hold life by the scruff of the neck?
Scorning all that you once used to agree.
Ignorance is bliss, discretion the better part of valour-
Maxims that betray what you tried to be,
Faith in longevity and its soul-engrossing violence
Make their way down to the sea.

Neglecting tradition, passing by the works of the sun
Makes you appreciate, at last, the light.
You don't weep for the weak, nor speak for the voiceless,
You remain unmoved by their plight.
To voice unchained emotions for the sake of the truth,
Your life remains unchanged in your sight.
If compassion was once ingrained into your hardened soul,
Then kindness has walked away into the night.

54. The Poet And The Woman

The poet and the woman share the same kind of pain.
One wrapped in self-announced glory,
The other throwing away her innocence in vain
Waiting till it's all hunky-dory.

The poet's heart resembles a shattered jigsaw piece;
The woman has a soul of her own.
There's a reason neither can be at ease
At the seeds of discontent sown.

What's worrisome is that one shares them all the time,
While the other's never been heard to say.
Life's not meant to be fair, it's too hard a climb,
Yet they've both lost their way.

If one has no takers, the other has had too many;

The ghosts of friendly faces too few.
War stories to tell, experiences, if any
Have left them both without a clue.

I've heard them both recount their days of joy,
Saying they're now few and far between.
This widening grip of memory does destroy
And purify the crime at the scene.

The poet's heart is enveloped in profound grief
And the woman's in shame.
Anything that offers respite, however brief,
Might just put out this flame.

55. Too Soon It's Christmas

The fire is burning with a flame so red
That time stops ticking in your head.
Your soul has never been this aglow
And your body's never been inside the snow.
When you know Christmas is up ahead,
The days of pain seem to be of long ago.

Love has found another meaning this time,
Adding vertices to this climb.
Life has not known a phase of more delight;
'Stead of running away, you've begun to fight.
Peace seems as turbulent as wartime,
It's Christmas and you're sleeping well at night.

To be pleased with your efforts, to be free
To walk away into the wild or the sea.
God knows it's Christmas when you smile
And tell yourself it's OK to stay awhile.

There are reasons why you need to be
More patient to make it worthwhile.

The gift of time has found a meaning;
A half of it is awake and a half dreaming.
Incongruous of the praxis of your love
That's been accepted by the heavens above.
Of the things you need, desire is intervening
To remind you what it won't behove.

Life has escalated to the heights of dizzying feats
Yet it remains interred in heartbeats.
Too soon it's Christmas and you wonder aloud
Whether this year has made you proud.
Confident enough to know that history repeats
Itself; coming a full circle in this crowd.

What have you not given in this search you're on?
The night seems long before the dawn.
Yet all you can do is endure, take it if you must
Going back to the things and people you trust.

Now that it's Christmas and autumn is gone,
There's a reason it's YOU they chose to entrust.

56. Assurance

Now if it were to come to a test
What we, in our lives, miss the most,
Every wave that touches our coast
Didn't make it to the standard boast
Of our conquests, when it almost
Starts to abut itself in this quest.

Now if it were to come to a toss
As to what would have been, had we not met
On these shores, when you began to fret
Having missed the boat. And I let
You worry not knowing the truth yet
That I would have swum you across.

Would it have hurt if I helped you cross
The sea with all its bitter tides?
Nothing worse than the slides
We would have had and besides
By then we would have made strides

Neglecting triumph, being at a loss.

57. Oh, Little Butterfly

Little butterfly, why can't you be
Something more than my fantasy?
Why can't you fly out of the hole
That life has cut from your soul?
When you can fly no more
Do you wish for a life like before?

The corpses of men with broken
Dreams lie unmentioned, unspoken
Before the remains of men with hate
Washing their sins in the spate
Of the river that gave them birth
But pushes them back to the earth.

Such innocence finds no place today
When insecurity is here to stay
Camping deep inside my heart's walls.
But at night, when the lark calls
Probing me to savour this pain,

I can't know if it's a boon or a bane.

58. Unrequited Memory

Of the things that make a memory
Which are the ones that seek to be
More than a blur in your mind?
Which are the ones that are confined

To the wall that has our names?
Now that the city's up in flames,
What is it you want to see?
Do you, now, at least agree

To the terms laid down by life?
This endless, unloving strife
Has fulfilled the promises it kept.
Do you even try to accept

That memory is a cruel friend?
If only you had seen the bend

In the road when you tried to flee,
We could have shared this equally.

Romantic Leftovers

59. Our Poem

(1)
We're ensconced in this envelope of grief
As the strings of consolation tug us
At where it hurts the most. We're lying
Awake on top of each other like
Clouds waiting with bated breath
For another faithless, minuscule second
Before bursting onto the earth
With relentless fury. We're both too tired

To play this game of life and death.
Love had made a chance appearance
Somewhere in the middle but we
Misplaced it along with the best
Intentions of all our friends who said
That this was a mistake.
I smile with an unrepentant passion
Because they aren't here with us now.

(2)
This moment has had its fair share
Of glory and failure just as you and I
Have had ours. Our poem should be
Written on the whimsies of disappointment
And the dishonesty of time;
Not upon the ink-stained approval
Of unimaginative, discursory glances
From people who abhor the poetry of love.

Our poem was conceived when you took
My hand and led it towards the stars.
It was imagined when you waited no more
To take my breath away with fanfare.
It was composed when we were bound into this life.
Our poem was written when the wind blowing
Over the sunset remarked at everything
That we had left unsaid.

(3)
The world has left its indelible mark
On the memory of the moment we shared
And the magic of the various sources

Of love we had preserved ourselves from.
Our poem survived the intricacies
Of disapproval and all its uncooperative allies;
It held on to the mutability of laughter
And cried at the songs of hurt and longing.

Our poem was not ours alone;
It was of every inch of hopelessness
Prescribed deep into the trunk of faith.
It was of every tiny bit of perspiration
On your naked face before you
Put your blood-smeared mascara
Of attachment on.
I looked out of the window.

60. Three Easy Steps

What seems remarkably easy at first-
This dispassionate, impartial withdrawal
From the remnants of what we used to be
Gets a little wearisome as the day wears on,
Reminding me of the titbits that had
Kept me glued to you and your fantasies.

It's not withdrawal from you as such
But alienation from your ghosts-
The ones which had followed me
Everywhere I had gone and refused
To keep me where the light was;
It gets a tad difficult after this.

It will be delightful at first,
Walking away from what you had demanded
Me to be, although it might be tragic
Years later when we bump into each
Other. I would say nothing to you,

Nor you to me, but we'd both know.

What would happen when and if
I finally find the courage to pull the plug?
Would the dark clouds hovering above
This mountainous, darkened city choose
To vent their fury upon a hapless me?
I can't expect myself to understand.

In step one, I forget that I was yours
And you were mine. We disentangle ourselves
From this devious and dishonest hole
We had walked into. I disremember where we
Had met and when we had found
Refuge in this thing called love.

In step two, I say goodbye to your things,
The ones that had kept me company
Even when you had chosen to drift
Apart from the cocoon we had once
Concealed ourselves in; I keep forgetting

To ask you how you've been. It's just as well.

In the final step, I fail to brave up to
The memories that stand between us
And the future; the sour aftertaste of a
Hate-filled propensity springs up mid-conversation.
There is nothing tangible to be left behind,
Least of all the shouting matches.

All that we can agree upon is that
Nothing could have failed us better than
This life of togetherness we had chosen.
In an ironic twist of fate, it has come to
The fact that I don't remember what
Your name is anymore, nor you mine.

61. Rainbow

It had grown dark at first
Before it started to rain
Reminding us of how lucky we were
To be standing on this doorstep with
A roof above our heads and an
Indomitable distance between us.
Yes, this must have been the door
Where I used to wait so patiently.

The rains lashed out with a fury
That was unmatched for the wrath
And heartbreak they embodied.
Either they were standing by me for being
Unable to tell you what I wanted to
Or they were being unprejudiced in
Their ability to erode a part of history
You and I shared.

It felt difficult to rustle up the nerve

To mourn for what we had lost or even
Find out where our hearts had been
Flung deep into the sea.
How tough would it have been to
Find ourselves in this bedlam?
It felt harder not to tell you
What love had already decided for us.

Diving into the deepest of depths
To find a part of us that betrayal
And her sisters had misappropriated.
Courageous for having loved you,
Fortunate to have been loved by you.
It seemed as relevant a moment as any
To wonder that if a rainbow was what we wanted,
Perhaps our time had come.

62. Sleeping Of Stealth

It begins as a drop on a clear-headed day
Jogging towards the eventuality of summer,
Murmuring dissent within its all-encompassing
Cloud burst that knows no target.

Then it moves towards the matters of the heart
Inching closer to the inevitability of death,
Clutching at the dying embers of this edifice
As strongly as one would one's ripped-off head.

You turn to look towards me with a hint of
Fascination in your eyes and I struggle to worry,
Pushing behind all that had held us together.
I eke out a living by persisting on your trenches.

It would be nice to sit down someday,
Take due note of the happenings that shaped us

And wonder too, at what might have conspired
If that thing called love had assailed us in due course.

It would be fruitful to question, too,
If you ever thought of me the way I did of you.
Or if you ever attended to my misgivings in
A manner that would have befitted a saint.

And now it wants centre-stage, lurking behind
The shadows having got to its nerves after all.
Love was a simple thing indeed, no wonder
We let it run rings around us while we were asleep.

What it asks for now is a place in our memories,
Something that not even the most fortuitous glances
Which passed between us have merited. Yet it begs
For permission as if we hadn't heard it the first time.

It now moves towards the edges of our

Combined conscience, creeping stealthily onward
As we sit by the fire reminiscing and wondering,
Just wondering at what might have been.

63. When It's Your Birthday

When it's your birthday and all you can think of is the past,
Then the time has come for this question to be asked-
Why would you feel so despondent as the tears forcefully pull
And splurge today's pleasures? Why look at the glass half-full?

You're here today, on your feet, and stronger than before.
Life is full of joyful sunrises that leave you wanting for more.
If yesterday's ghosts leave you hurting to the core,
Then look at those faces in the light whom you adore.

There are the timid truths of life that you can never ignore;
The least you can do this moment is not be swept ashore.
Do your best to cling on to the rocks and try not to abhor
The memory of the one who left you wilting on the floor.

There's so much to be glad for, so many delights to be enjoyed.

Look towards tomorrow and have these ordeals destroyed.
There's no need for the limelight, just take time to applaud
The idea of who you are as today you are closest to God.

• 159 •

64. Miyapur

There used to be a window which opened inwards here.
Now rust has made itself comfortable and the shadows that
Fall along its landings have decayed past recognition.
There also used to be an old semi-detached around the corner;
There are still marked cornices that tell me of the remnants

Of its old residents: man, wife, kids and the old fox terrier.
There are no signs of you or our foreboding evenings here
Though; I often wonder if you chose to take them with you
To the place that you now call home to share with the man
You now call lover. There's also this old familiar sound

Which makes me turn around hoping against hope
For a miracle which would have made my widest exploits
proud.
There is no sign of you in my memories, though. I often feel
that
Either they have been wilfully omitted or erased completely
To prevent me from going on such wild goose chases.

The street calls itself by another name now; there is still the
old
Cafe with a huge cauldron full of Irani chai waiting to be
poured
Down the confines of my throat: gurgling yet as tepid as
Our love once used to feel. There is also the cinema hall
At the crossroads where we had never been, only thought of

Escaping from the incarcerations that other friends had
Put us into. How deeply this reflects upon you and the locale
Of Miyapur I do not know, yet I have had my time in the sun
as
I could not have loved you more than a man loves a woman
Whom he seldom sees, only writes to. That was not to be.

65. Mid-Sea Tragedy

Why there cannot be any sanity in this madness I will never know.

It's perhaps ornamenting to the cause of the bedlam I have created.

Too tangible, too derogatory to be worthy of a mention;
Have I crossed all limits that civil society had written so brightly
About in the dispatches that were sent home?

What's worse is the beginning of this perfectly simple candlelit dinner
Wherein all I can see are your glowing lips and perfectly curled eyelashes.
I shiver with grief recollecting the times I had made you feel that I was
Indeed in love with you, and rejoiced at the feeling that you were 'me'.
How quickly did this love-stricken ship of ours start to drift?

Whence did this lovable back-and-forth become a game of
chess?
Two participants, dressed in black as the entire town mourned
at the loss
Of a cause gone sour, trying to feel the joy in such situations,
trying to
Alter it at the same time, resulting in having un-felt whatever
it was
That had brought me towards your terracottean shores.

To be malleable enough to fit into the column this world has
marked out
For me and my now-infamous antics, to be harmless enough
to work my
Way out of the tragic hole I so often find myself burrowed in-
how do I
Know where to draw the line? Frightened at the prospect of
facing you,
I choose the easier way out and tell her it's over.

66. Post Mortem

Now that I've successfully managed to drive you away,
Will you remember me only by the pretentious bits that
Still come back to haunt me, or will you recollect those
Days of warmth when nothing but the absolute truth
Used to pass between us? What will your heart tell you
In the dark of the night when the contours of my breathing
Are no longer able to assist and guide you to bed?

Will you ever be able to imagine yourself with another man?
Will you be able to look him in the eye and speak about
The great deceitful game that we had played, or will you
Hesitate in telling him about your troubled past? Do his eyes
Twinkle when he talks about his hopes and his dreams? Will
such
Conversations rebut into my being inside your being again,
And will they give you comfort when the winds of pain blow?

What will you make of the fleeting undercurrents of love
That floated between our shores in the barren sands of time?

Will they have given you enough faith to never trust a man
Again, or will they have made you understand up to where
The tentacles of my cowardice extended? Will you remain on
My Christmas card list, or join the long list of girls who had
Suffered from the same ordeal before and did not understand?

Why did it not work? Was it because of the stubbornness with
Which I greeted the existence of us transpiring? Two bodies-
One soul and all the promises that your friends had made, will
you
Now vouch for the fact that love's tentacles can be crueller
than death's?
For me, I don't think I can ever go to the Lake without feeling
The tuft of your hair within the expanses of my loneliness
And the setting sun suggesting to me that you're still listening.

67. Old Flame

I couldn't recognise it although the name matched yours.
Too much mascara and that you'd never have worn red
Reinforced my feeling, yet there was no doubt it was you.
Touched-up aplenty and speaking a thousand words,

It jumped out at me, screaming 'The Sexiest Woman in the City!'
I wouldn't have believed it if I hadn't seen the familiar
Tilt of the head and the incongruous smile, feeling lost
In the dizzying world of glamour and its acolytes.

It doesn't hurt much these days, although I did
Feel a throbbing pain in my head after I saw it.
How long has it been? Long enough for me to forget what
You smelt like and not long enough for you to remember

To wear the bracelet I had given to you on your eighteenth.

I read that you keep that room as a studio somewhere east-
Is it to escape from your newly-found family life,
Or as a token of remembrance for lovers past?

I couldn't understand why you had to flush your skin
With the toxins that were meant to slowly kill you
Or why you'd felt the need to doll up so much so that
Your eyelashes crumpled under the pain of neglect.

The creases on your forehead looked prolonged and you
Appeared flustered by the weight of fame upon your
shoulders.
When my wife stepped into the room, I was quick to
Tear the page in half and throw the tabloid away.

68. The Room On The Roof

The noise of the creaking of the ceiling fan
Stopped when you stopped being in love with me.
It was robust when you were, and inert

When you weren't, and I was compelled to switch it off.
Nothing seemed to be wrong but there was
Always the fear of getting crushed underneath.

It felt different when the stars were lit in joy on a clear sky
Ornamented by the jealous glares of the moon.
We always tried to avoid such petty confrontations

Trying to preserve this sanctum sanctorum.
Hatred spewed its vile juices in the living room
But Envy was quiet enough to polish it unabashedly.

I wonder if you listen to the noise of the creaking
Of the ceiling fan in your room adorned by posters of a
sulking
Sandra Oh, or if you choose to sleep through the fracas.

Does the sky ever look you in the eye with mercy askance?
When it rains, I feel the drops of happenstance
Seep through the roof, unable to bat an eyelid amid the
bedlam.

69. After Years Of Hearsay

It's not as if we were designed to be
Walking hand in hand along the sea.
Nor were the words we spoke ever free
Of the allusions we meant them to be.
It wasn't that difficult for us to agree
That it was time we got off this tree.

You told me that you didn't want to go there
As it reminded you of a sordid affair.
Lucky enough to have avoided the scare,
We held hands as we murmured a prayer.
The sight we saw that day was so rare
That we walked straight into thin air.

We didn't sign a contract of love in Bombay
But that didn't stop me from asking you to stay.
Telling myself that I wasn't leading you astray
Wasn't easy when you had my faith to betray.
We'll meet again after years of hearsay.

Surely, our love will endure this delay.

70. Surrender

It's autumn, and we've joined hands once again
Trying to force a way through this wall
Of incoherence that fills our days.
Where are we going to go from here?
Several hundred places, several hundred faces.

A cackle of expectation as we raise our arms
In deference. This leads to our meek capitulation
And resignation before our bolder selves.
The sun's rays line up in all their glory
Pushing ignorance to streets of disrepair.

And now you say that you're leaving Telangana,
Disrespecting this tangle of arms and legs
And the semi-united persona we have become.
The corners of this alley illuminate the night
As we get caught in the crossfire.

Whose undercurrents pass through our banks?
Are they of a mild and obliging temperature
And do they rush through in great brevity?
You had once told me that you wanted
To be loved; now we're mid-air.

Two passengers in this endless journey
With Time and its docile sycophants
Who know better than to ask you to stay.
I sometimes wish that I had their acquiescence,
Planting a kiss on your eager cheeks.

Crossing borders has never seemed easier
Because it is not just love that has
Ploughed its way deep into the essence
Of our lives. The ways of this gentle heart
And abstinent soul remain unthanked.

71. You Have A Decision To Make

Let me tell you why I chose this road
Over the one which by my side flowed.
This fabric heart seeks a pagan love-
One that hasn't yet been heard of.
I had been reluctant at first
As the envelope of certainty burst.

The rain clouds up my windowpane
'Til nothing but questions remain.
The answers to which have never
Been asked nor dwelt upon whatsoever.
I ask for decency and comfort to give
And the strength to forgive.

When I have waited for you for half a year
And you seem farther away, not near,
That's it! This is all that I have to give.
And hey, this is surely no way to live.

Take me back to the sunset by the lake-
God, I feel so tired and my bones ache.

This seems like a torrid night in the sea
When we've experienced the joy of being free.
But what goes on inside your mind when
You think of me and force a smile again?
The sun is setting along our side of the lake,
It's a pity you have a decision to make.

72. This Existential Crisis

This entanglement of arms and legs- this precision
Of them being exactly where I want them to be-
This very proposal of our existence being questioned-
This withdrawal of our selfish selves- this reluctance and
This recalcitrance- this whataboutery- these sleepless nights.

Of all days we choose today- of all chances we take
The ones that have befallen us now- of early mornings
And even earlier nights- of asking ourselves the same
Questions- of being surprised at how they yield different
Answers at different times of the day- of pretending to enjoy
it.

This inquest of the death of whatever we shared- this
Multiplicity of evil clouds overhead- this vagabonding
Of the tendencies of love- this disinclination and this
Retreat of your lips- this cajoling of my fingertips-
The installation of my hands upon your eager ones.

Of hinting at multiple possibilities- of insinuations
And its cruel friends in tow- of limiting ourselves
To just a peck- of wandering through the woods declaring
Ourselves to be the first to have encountered this feeling-
Of reassuring with a smile that everything will be alright.

73. Yesterday You Were Here With Me

Do you ever feel the stars shine just for you?
Or do you put that down to another tragic
Coincidence that binds us for the few
Days of laughter and years of magic?

Do you get to know when I miss you?
Do you feel the warmth of this winter sun?
It goes into hiding as if on cue,
Walking away coolly when it's done.

Does your cheek ever throb in dispute
And leave you longing for my skin?
The pining for your touch gets acute
In places where you have not been.

We loved like there was no tomorrow,

Wading in and out of destiny's arms.
Yet fate gave us such pleasures of sorrow
When the night wore away all its charms.

How lethargic have we become
For our hearts to stop and take notice
Of why we are numbered under the sun?
It's sadder still to get to know this.

Your presence has a grace of its own;
Your smell distinctive by its voice.
Showering us with what we've known-
Of remarks that left us with no choice.

The fads of time can't be understood
As we stand enjoying a love this free.
I try hard to forget that, as I should,
Yesterday you were here with me.

There isn't much to which I agree;
Not with emotions that are as base.
These warm winds that embrace me
Must have surely kissed your face.

74. Cephalalgia

When these frosty winds take a break
From trying to change the way they blow
And the lights upon this road are aglow,
Hardly a soul is left stirring in their wake.
You and I are forced to forego
The intimacy we want to know.

We exchange a look of challenge in our eyes.
You say what I don't want to hear.
Languishing on top of my deepest fear
Is when love visits in disguise.
Yet, to this day, we're nowhere near
To shake off a cephalalgia as severe.

The enormous shore of your hair
Seeks comfort in my willing hands.
Yet I gently obey their commands;
Letting you go would not be fair.
You and I meet in the wastelands

Fulfilling each other's demands.

You take the heartbreak of the sunrise well
Just as I make my way out the door.
I am cold and shaken to the core
To see the breaking of this spell.
The cat waves 'bye curled on the floor
As the ripples of time sweep me ashore.

I liked you well enough to be able to see
How my leaving didn't come as a blow.
It reminded me of a time not long ago
When we had been anchored to the sea;
You seemed like the sempiternal glow
Of a land I did not want to know.

75. Just A Pantomime

Let us imagine a place where you and I like
Each other's company and walk hand in hand
To wherever it is that we have to go, and are
Not scared of the curious stares of women
In your neighbourhood and the voyeuristic
Glances of people who can not be like us.

I have often told you that love is imperfect
And it is its flaws that makes us so real
In a world filled with make-believe.
You have seldom listened, if you have at all,
To those monologues of mine
That began and ended with John Mayer.

You don't believe me when I say that this is
What I want; that this is the chance that I
want to take. It seems to be a pity to me
That you perceive the world to be just as you
Assume it to be. I can't accuse you of being

Narrow-minded; just too restricted.

How I would have loved to show you it wasn't so
If you had given me the chance, and how
I would have loved to hear you rant about your
Former lovers who stay hidden deep inside your
Heart. I say nothing as you wrap my fingers around
Yours and tell me that love can never be flawless.

I am just about to say what it is that I would
Like us to do when I remember that perhaps this
Seems to be a tiny game to you, waiting as you
Are for him to phone back and apologize.
I feel sorry for myself; these months you
Led me astray could have been fruitful otherwise.

I must not make mental calculations without
Speaking to you first but it is such a shame
That this thing we shared was just a pantomime.
When I struggle to afford the luxury of sleep
Some nights, I wonder if it was he who broke you

Or if I had not been able to mend what was left.

76. To You, On New Year's Day

I wish upon you good health and more happiness
Than I could ever perceive as possible to give
To you. To be able to sneak perchance into the
Possibilities that we had thought outlandish,
To be able to walk away unattached from the
Growing pains of this lingering darkness-
In the year ahead, I hope you have the light.

These glances of inhuman distances that
Have crossed our paths now may have been
Painted specifically to prevent you from holding my hand.
If only love was there to guide our stars when
We had lain unaware of the protocols of this
Flirtationship; we broke them quite often.
When your eyes seek mine and I am unable

To give you the reassurance that his welcoming
Smile does, the wind howls in laughter inside my ears.

How difficult must it be to let the words out in the open,
To allow the freezing gusts of despair wrap its
Arms around your knees and beg for forgiveness?
I hope you have peace and the ability to look
At me impartially but not dispassionately this year.

I hope that you give everything that you have to give
To the one you love, and I do not ask that to be me,
For I have long understood and escaped from the confines
Of such ultimata that have gripped our insides.
These insides burn with a fire which must
Not be doused, and I hope you never have to pour
Water upon the flame of love that you glow upon.

You look beautiful even when you walk away
From me, and I surmise that it would remain
So even when I have forgiven the crimes that
Passion and its synonyms had alleged upon me.
If I had the strength to give, then I would have
Gladly made room for the acquiescence with
Which you stood up and asked me not to stay.

Whatsoever became of the promises we made,
Whatever is left of them have now long disappeared
To the realms of an inordinately cold, windswept autumn.
It is winter now, and although it won't stay that
Way for long, I have every reason to believe
That the moment when our fingertips touched,
It did not mean anything to you at all.

Whatever hollow guarantees we have remaining
Glance furtively at my early morning overtures,
And I hope you never have to know what I think of
When I walk past your house when you lie sleeping.
And of course, like Vikram Seth, I hope that the sun
Burns my footprints on your lawn, and holds
You continually in its warmth and keeping.

77. Multicolour

A look of defiance, a well-meaning question
Almost escapes from your lips before it gets cut off.
Does it feel sinful to look at me in this condition?
Or does the pride in your already sinking chest
Swell through the lac-filled outer covering
And ask for something very close to forgiveness?
Of all the things that you have seen me become,
This might be the hardest to digest.
What ever happened to those nights we spent
On the grass gazing at the stars and counting
Our blessings, what ever happened to the endless
Glasses of water poured down our reluctant throats
As we sought a place called freedom away from
The hate-filled dispensers that our families had become?
When it appears to you that you can not take it
Any more and need to sit down and catch your breath
Whilst reliving the days of our past,
Always remember that I was there before you were,
Losing myself in this hideous process. Reinventing
The cores of something that then resembled
These exposed skeletons trespassing the
Outer limits of this thing called 'our friendship.'

78. We Share The Sadness

The truth appears harsher in the light
And once we have escaped from time,
We still hold on, frantically trying to unify
Those pieces of our souls which were lost
In the process of redefining a life from
Amongst the broken shards of despair.

We knew this day would come,
We knew it all along even though we
Tried to act otherwise and tell
Ourselves anecdotes that would have
Taken away the verities of experience.
Love was unfair, but life was not.

But how are we supposed to bequeath
That which has become of us now?
How are we supposed to share this sadness
That has engulfed the horizons which
We both inhabit but try to run away

From? Don't blink when you open your

Eyes to the rude cruelties of what we
Could have become if only we had paid
Heed to what the wind, fire and the sun
Were trying to tell us. Alas, we had been
Nestled too deep for far too long inside
The chrysalis we thought would never break.

Sometimes I wonder if you think of me
When I think of you, and if you feel the passing
Trace of things left unsaid and memories
Left untouched. Or if you feel the wind kissing
Your face with the desperate yearning
Of the embrace we had once shared.

It might be the only time we both feel
This sadness that threatens to run amok
The green expanses of delight that you
Have built for yourself. Does it ever occur
To you that you never once asked me

What I felt; never once turned back?

I used to fight with the Gods to slow the
Hands of the clock down whenever
You were around. It's tragic that you could
Not feel even a bit of the temptation
That passed between our fingertips.
How could it not have moved you?

I wonder if the tempestuous intensity
With which I stare towards the direction
Where your house lies in the unforgiving
Morning light might break into your
Sleep, let you know that I am thinking of you
And somehow tell me that you're alright.

I want to know if you see the stars
Tonight like I do, as it might be my
Only right left consecrated upon you.
We have shared chunks of happiness
And all its metonyms before, so it's only fair

That tonight, we share this sadness.

79. Promises, Promises

I lie down beside the grave of the promises we made
Amid the bedlam that your intention to leave has
Created. We have reached the safety that
The years can claim to have built- so unfulfilled
That nothing can declare to be a part of us.

All that I thought had slipped past me in the
Old sieve of disjointed and discredited memories
Are swelling up in hubris at the mention of your
Thoughtlessness. Whence did this shameful
Feeling of mesmerising rancour barge its way in?

There is no succour in knowing that the future
Might lie somewhere east of where we stand today.
How do you expect me to tell myself that the sun,
Trying to be as meek as possible to set amongst
The ebbing tides, has finally claimed us as its own?

Inching past the hope that tomorrow brings
And the gloom that our years together delivers,
Will I find the strength to say goodbye?
I wish I had been strong enough to tell you that
I wanted you to stay, and that you looked beautiful

Even when the tears smeared your sleek
Mascara down those honey-rimmed eyes.
These moments will last longer than the love
That consumed us in its spectral fire,
Like the promises we so seldom broke.

80. Dream Of Me

Light no longer comes in filtered rays
Through the door where I used to wait
So patiently that it took up all my days.
Pushing gently towards the sins of Fate,

I've been past the spot where we embraced
With a twinge of nostalgia and regret.
All those shiny dreams that I chased
Resolutely tie me in their debt.

I've been to the Lake once or twice by now
Haunted by the intimacy we reached.
It hasn't taken me long to wonder how
Your indifference was never breached.

Thoughts in my unguarded moments have crept
And found their way to your house by the sea.

I'm not sure you'll find it easy to accept-
When you're not asleep, you dream of me.

Residues Of The Heart

81. Equity

You said you'd dreamt of me
And since there is equity,
I have felt much the same
Tug when it came to claim
That unhinged, untangled sin
Debarred from within
But expressed all the same.
Hence love in all but name
Has found its way towards our
Souls at this ungodly hour
By making eye contact from
Juries that rendered numb
Those feelings which, in effect,
Seem treacherous in retrospect.

You speak of faith and trust
And yes, indeed you must
Rejoice what came to you
Gifted, packed as brand-new.
But remember what you must
Do to settle, and perhaps adjust

If it comes to that, but don't blame
Yourself if you fail; the aim
Of this is to ask if you would give
More than you receive, and forgive
Me if I make inquiries
Around time's well-kept diaries.
And ask yourself- since there's equity,
Do you deserve a poem from me?

82. Ships Passing In The Night

Like the cloud which loomed but did not burst,
Or the storm that did not come
So far aground to quench my thirst;
You asked me where I was from.

I didn't foresee seeing you that night,
Not when I had been so far.
From what I was trying to write,
Piety gave way to empathy in the bazaar.

We knew the rules, yet we signed up to play
As dangerous a game as the one we did.
Yet love's tentacles have led me astray
Past the senses our hearts so well hid.

Let dusk settle on my desk for one more day,

As I experience what only the idle can afford-
The luxury of seeking you when you're not away,
Knowing that you'd acquiesce and be on board.

If I could, I would have held you in such a tight
Grip that you wouldn't have left the door ajar.
For you, I wasn't just a ship passing by in the night,
Nor for me were you merely a shooting star.

I have tried to not miss you dearly. Oh, I should
Try to walk away from the faint beams of love.
It has been just the way you said it would-
At that moment, it did not seem as tough.

What else was desired of this meeting
Of the poet and a seeker of the truth?
It hasn't been so tempting as to repeating
On a warm summer night a walk as smooth.

It was remarkably subtle, difficult to apprehend.

When the sun was setting yesterday,

I wished you'd been there to see it end

But I mention that only by the way.

83. That This Is So

Take my hand, and guide it past the residues
Of these brilliantined escapades that the sunshine
Has written its name on today; fake sincerity
And tell me that you have never felt this way before.
Escort me beyond the lines where civility ends
And past the boundaries where the modern
Confines of our lives merge seamlessly into the
Path towards your oft-darkened and misconstrued
Soul; leave me in the gloom waiting to smell the
Roses on a day when you get engulfed in the madness.

Wake me before this tragic happening of our
Disjointed feelings run unabashedly among the gardens
Of pecuniary worship. The clouds gather overhead
Amidst the noise of an azure Hyderabadi sky that
Expels all notions of me being shut deep within the
Immurements of your fingertips. Touch me and tell me
That this is real, and that this is so- that love and life
Blend illogically in a country where the Gods reside.
It would be far too difficult to accept the actualities
That our alter egos have imposed upon us.

84. The Golden Hour

I wait for you in our golden hour,
Day after day, week after week.
I know not if I want to hear from you;
Lesser still do you want to hear from me.
And yet I wait for you in the golden hour,
Day after day, week after week.

Not a day goes by when I don't think of you,
More so in this golden hour of ours,
Which was truly ours and could be no one else's,

Unlike those promises we had bent with unfettered will.
What can I do to recant those absurd words
That my mouth had disclosed that doomed night?

There has been no golden hour since then,
But I light up in expectation whenever

I hear that old familiar sound and hope that
It's you when I turn around. There's no way of
Knowing if you wait for me in the golden hour,
Or if you feel that peculiar tug too.

85. The Concluding Statement

I see you peeping through the door.
In your restlessness, I see
The opulence that you once wore,
The remnants of a final plea.
As to the magnificence of the floor
And the naiveté that I adore,
Alas, I've bent too much at the knee
And grovelled; I hope you agree

That things are better the way they are-
You and I divided by this subtle line
Marking us distinct from afar.
If only I had seen the sign.
There is no need for us to spar
When we have coasted so far
From the shore we tried to define
And surrender in the sunshine.

You look extremely sad, and I fear
That the days left are too few.
But there's nothing really to cheer
To, as you bid adieu
To the abscesses of me that you hold dear
To the grips and claws of this frontier.
I know for a fact you feel it too-
That I am not in love with you.

86. In Continuation

I am not in love with you
But a part of me wishes I were.
Or if I'd been in love with her
This severance would've held true.
Or if I'd jumped off this train
And saved you a lot of pain.

I will always choose to look
With constant ease at the light.
When separation was in sight
This painful road that we took
Drove us towards sorrow's eye
In full force. If you ask why

Was it that I chose to see
The fears that yesterday brought
With the dreams that we bought
And imprinted in my memory,
I'd say it's never easy; always dry.

The shock grows the more you try.

87. Faithless Timidity

The tilting of your head to the sky,
The light in your eyes still aglow,
We two
Well knew
That it was not too long ago
When we had this contact high.

What were those words you said
As I painlessly surveyed your face?
Of course
The coarse
Lines on your fingers leave no trace
Of animosity or loving. We're ahead

Of the curve that defines who we are
And limits who we set out to be.
It would,
As it should,
Matter much less than what we see.

"Please open the door of the car!"

"I can't! I have to go to work tomorrow.
And it's been too late already."
Without ease,
I freeze.
And with the finger on my lips unsteady
Search for undeserving sorrow.

88. The Blinking Sun

Of course, it would be easier still
To let me pick and choose the kill
And ask you for a chance
That seems naive at first glance.
But who will sow the seeds of love?

In a heart terrified of alien touch
Afraid to spend itself too much?
Pain stings the umbrae of my eyes.
It's clear that you can't give me lies
Though push has now come to shove.

I may have sold myself. It's true
That you felt I was in love with you.
You knew it when you saw my grief
And tried to give me some relief.
But soon it came from above

And made you turn away from me.
I have no chains now. I am free
To walk away from these doors
That reek of everything that's yours.
But I am still knee-deep in hurt

And I suspect you feel the same.
Now the wildflowers are aflame
From love sprinkled with envy.
It's time to serve exile upon me
And heed that early alert.

When the sun has set, I look to see
What the dusk has brought for me.
There is no sentience. Nor is there light.
In the relentlessly unloving night,
The sun tries to blink in the dirt.

89. The Aftermath

When the poem I wrote on the clouds
Found its way to you by the sea,
It was easy to forget all my doubts.
No sense of duty, nor cheering crowds
Could have granted such ecstasy.
In your wrinkled brows, I could see

An apology for things you had not done,
Penitence for words you did not mean.
The joy was not after the day was won
Nor were the stories that we spun
By friendship, love, and everything in between.
What, in fact, had we been?

I look back at those days with no joy
And avoid whatever I know you can sense.
It's harder to build something than destroy,
Which, to our chagrin, we found. Oh boy,
Life seems dubious without evidence;

It isn't easy to let go of this pretence.

90. Far From The Dark

Whenever I see your agitated face,
At its docility, I express some dismay
Within. It would've been hearsay
Had I laughed at what I didn't admit.
I console you dishonestly. Do sit
And eat your dinner with some grace.

I cannot hope to make you see
What I aim to bring to this dishonoured
World nor are you to be bothered
To ask what goes inside my head.
It's at its last dredge now- this thread
That ties us. I am free.

Free to escape from this dark,
Pitiless and unclean room
With its tones of impending doom.
You don't read poetry, nor I eat cakes-
It's truly a shame. It takes

Two to walk hand-in-hand in the park.

91. A Rare Sight Of You

To be, unknowingly, at odds and ends,
To forget how to make amends,
I must have lost track of time
Being on that wobbly, rocky climb.
But it was no doubt a sight of you
Today in the serpentining queue.

You had the same shoes on your feet
As you did when we last could meet.
The hair tied into a ponytail
The skin was sallow yet not pale.
The frame upright with rigid grace
Involuntarily, I slowed my pace.

I half expected you to turn your face,
Prove me right and then embrace.
But when you did so, I shook
Having so painfully mistook
One who seemed to have all your traits.

No crueller joke was played by the fates.

92. If You're Reading This, It's Too Late

If you're reading this, it's too late.
Especially if you're doing so under
Sheaves of sodden flowers
Tainted with the filth that our love
Brought in its wake. If you're mad at
Me now for choosing to write after
Months of denying and making excuses,
I don't blame you.

The stain that the dingy leaves
Of the late monsoon have brought in
Its aftermath lingers deeper than
The solace that your memories bring.
There is no joy in knowing that I
Had once known you, or loved
You more passionately than a man
Had ever loved a woman.

There is no shame that the long
Unfulfilled touch of desire that
Resides deep inside our personae
Has not expressed. Who were we
To question the cowardice that the
Waves of time and coasts of relief
Brought upon our edgeless swords?
I hope you're well.

I had heard from well-meaning friends
About how you retreated into yourself
And spoke of nothing in confinement.
I was no doubt sure that such captivity
Could only breed hostility of the highest
Order. Hence, my inability to accord
You with acknowledgements can
Never be forgiven.

I will do well to steer clear of begging
For your forgiveness, because even
If you make the mistake of doling
It out to me, I do not deserve you.
I would not have held the quaking

Of the clouds inside my chest
If I had known that you were
Soon to come home.

My failings have failed to drive home
The fact that your inadequacies
Were the only blankets that
Kept my sanity intact in this bedlam
Of broken hearts. Yet, I choose
To disown and disappropriate
Whatever it was that tied me to you.
I apologise profusely.

Our love was the creation of destiny
And its offshoot was the tenderness
That enveloped my lips long
After you made your exit.
This letter will no doubt find you
Trembling with anticipation. I just hope
That it reaches you in time before
You reach out for your pills.

If this doesn't touch a nerve, I don't
Know what will. The cascading of
This gentle moonbeam on your
Hesitant skin and my serenading
Your taciturn fingers bring back
A tear or two to these grime-stained
Partitions of our longing. No monsoon
Can wash the pain of these hearts away.

93. What You Tried To Say

Now when I think of you,
I do so without regret.
For a while, it was a threat
I'd have been in your debt.
Thankfully it's not so bad as yet
Although I do not have a clue

As to what it could have been
That made you turn away
With such distaste that every ray
Of the sun turned to grey.
Now I know what you tried to say-
Thanks for never coming clean.

94. Your Broken Heart

And since it is my wont to say
That I won't let my tears fray
Or be as bold to suggest, if I may,
To be sorry at the end of the day.
But it does not appear too hard to try
To push it away on its own, by and by.

It wasn't more than what we
Had expected of that night. Be
It my garrulity, or forsaken glee
At the fact that we could now be
Free to not see each other again,
And be spared of this glorious pain.

So it developed between two
Strangers that night what few
Would understand. Bid adieu
To the bitter plan that went askew
And lead me towards your broken heart.

Let me append that which was torn apart.

95. Supposed To Fall

In light of the night we spent
In the company of destiny's friends,
No curves in the road, nor any bends
Could have thrown us off the scent

That life gave to us in plain view.
I was not sure that I meant it when
I asked for your hand. But then
I had never seen anyone like you.

It was not easy to look you in the eye;
Harder still was to walk on that road
Where the gush of emotions flowed
And the pace of life didn't pass you by.

What would we have done, if at all
The winds of fate blew our way?

Lacking the courage to make you stay,
Were we both just supposed to fall?

96. The Winter Of Time

When you came, swift as the rain that never fell,
These glistening drops of dew tried their best to evade
The minute attention of my deepest yearnings.
How fortuitous it may have seemed to you

When it escaped the recognition of my ambitions.
These winds could not have avoided making
Themselves at home in the rut-covered abscesses
Of our one-laned, voluble conversations at night.

No incessant thunderstorm could have prevented
Me from looking deep inside the labyrinth that
Were your eyes, nor could any tragedy- natural or
Unnatural- let me run things down to a point

Where our passion got reduced to a bare trickle.
With what aspiration did we make the journey
Into the mysterious dusk, foraging for trust
Without so much as an umbrella to keep us dry?

Unbeknownst to you, life took a turn without
Us in tow. Had it really been that long that I last
Held your hand in mine, nibbled at your fingertips
Looking for the first signs of approval, whispered

Into your ears words that I thought you had
Always wanted me to say, run my hand through
The back of your neck while you involuntarily quivered
Envisioning a future filled with immeasurable joy?

Was it really that long ago that you gave up
In the fight to know for yourself what you meant
To me; when I tasted the desire that enveloped
Our still-beating hearts without the pernicious

Effects of fervid relief; when you trembled
As I touched your lips; when you looked me
In the eye and said all that was there to say.

How could time have wintered that away?

None of our belongings has withstood the autumn
Of our dreary existence, far from the arms we had
Once sought and obtained effortlessly. Secrecy pervades
Itself into my very being when I think of you;

My heart goes into raptures when you make
Appearances in my dreams but the mind stays still.
These clouds hover reluctantly to make themselves
Comfortable; I don't ask them to stay the night.

97. Bending The Rules

Maybe it won't be so bad, you and me-
Without the fun and frolic and revelry
Watching the sunset over the sea
Away from what we were presumed to be,
Lost in a realm solely our own. Free

From the nudity of someone else's eye
In a world held by the azure sky.
While we wait for love to pass us by,
I can, obscurely, hear you cry;
I lose sight of the edicts we could defy.

98. The Forgotten Ghost

If I can reek in the comfort and solace
Of the memories of a time so long ago,
Been chased away from that dreadful place,
Will it still come, to you, as a blow?
Will it remind you of the joy we sought
As history corrects the wars we fought?

If I speak to you, or of you, I do so with joy
And with a longing to see you again.
I don't proudly admit that I tried to destroy
The glee I found wrapped in pain
Without the appendage of your trust
Or the burden that floats in dust.

Did love ever visit our forsaken shores
Or were we only caught in between?
Why we made no sense of the closed doors
Of sentences, whether abrupt or mean
Is not difficult to understand now.

Were we doomed from the start somehow?

With no regret do I admit the fact
That I tried my best to see the way
The light comes in through the cracked
Glass on your window. While you sway,
The thistles outside try to wave me aside
And tell me how I hurt your pride.

All these clouds float along the coast
Of my unworthy obligations to you.
If you think of me as a forgotten ghost
Underneath everything that went through,
Then do not deprive me of your touch
Or the fact that you have seen too much.

If I choose reluctantly to melt away
Into the dirt of my sole window,
Then every flicker of light, and each array
Can have its share in the innuendo
About the vile designs and the base

Plans of the dream we had to chase.

The wind doesn't seem to let up at all
Nor does the reality of shadows.
In the bigger scheme of things, it may befall
Us to be aware of the way it blows.
They've been clipped at the wings;
These desires- such dreadful things!

Why life picked us to play this game
Is something I can never understand.
Innocence is something you try to claim
As you bashfully take my hand
And entwine it painlessly in yours.
I welcome you back to these doors.

Do you ever think of me these days
Or do you willfully choose to forget
The candour of our intolerable ways?
Now that your aims have been met,
Is 'home' still something of a shared dream

Of love, faith and everything in between?

99. My Progress Report

(I)

Will my necessity unravel with time, as I thought
It would? Or will I have to untie every knot
That your existence has blazoned in my heart?
It's true: love's harder when you're apart
Than when you're near, but I can now feign
To walk amongst the poplars in the rain.
It's easier too, to forget the hurt and the pain
That life has brought upon me and abstain
To digress upon that which has induced joy
To those eyes. It's easy enough to destroy
Every bit of sanity that I said would haunt
Me in my waking hours; it's easier still to flaunt
That I can now walk past those very doors
Upon which I had waited for hours. What's yours
Is yours and will remain so, and yet I can eye
The dark shadows under this cloudless sky
Without a hint of remorse or a twinge of regret.
Of course, it is simpler to pretend to forget.

(II)

I can now look at the hills in the distance
With a detachment that belies my very existence
Or pry upon the squirrels racing on these leaves.
The bulbul on my window ledge now grieves
For debris of the days of summers gone by.
A chord strikes inside me when I hear it cry
Reminding me that I haven't thought of you all day;
That's progress of some sort- of what I can't say.

100. Exit Poem

Since this tome has come to an end,
You will heave a sigh of relief.
The poet did try hard to befriend
You, and strangely, has kept this brief.

While this might seem like goodbye,
The author has no such plans at all.
There's more to this than meets the eye;
This book is for both big and small.

It's for you, you and you who can
Read till the end of this labour of love.
And you, who, instead chose to scan,
May God have mercy from above.

Acknowledgements

A lot of work has gone behind the scenes for this collection to come out. Apart from my team of editors and literary agents at Xpress, thanks are due in abundance to Aleesha Matharu, Prachi Batra and Pariplab Chakraborty for their constant encouragement in letting LiveWire become the second home to most of my creative pursuits.

www.ingramcontent.com/pod-product-compliance
Lightning Source LLC
Chambersburg PA
CBHW032014150726
47990CB00005B/1957